GONE BUT NOT FORGOTTEN

SEAGULL
BOOKS
·
CELEBRATING
40 YEARS

THE GERMAN LIST

HANS MAGNUS ENZENSBERGER

GONE BUT NOT FORGOTTEN

My Favourite Flops
and Other Projects That Came to Nothing

TRANSLATED BY MIKE MITCHELL

LONDON NEW YORK CALCUTTA

This publication has been supported by a grant from the Goethe-Institut India

Seagull Books, 2022

Originally published as Hans Magnus Enzensberge, *Meine Lieblings-Flops, gefolgt von einem Ideen-Magazin*
© Suhrkamp Verlag, Berlin, 2010

First published in English by Seagull Books, 2022
English translation © Mike Mitchell, 2022

ISBN   978 0 8574 2 977 3

British Library Cataloguing-in-Publication Data
A catalogue record for this book is available from the British Library.

Typeset by Seagull Books, Calcutta, India
Printed and bound in the USA by Integrated Books International

CONTENTS

Premises

'Flop' is a relatively new loanword in German and one that is highly acceptable, especially for the onomatopoeic quality ascribed to it by the OED. It is indispensable in show business but it serves well in other areas too.

The dull thud made by a flop is usually followed by a prolonged, audible silence. My dear fellow artists—whether writers, actors, painters, film-makers, singers, sculptors or composers—why are you so reluctant to talk about your minor or major failures? Is it embarrassment? Are you worried you might look foolish? But in that respect I can reassure you. From all the things you've told me in confidence, I conclude that I'm not the only one who has interesting flops and other failed projects to look back on. Otherwise I wouldn't be taking the trouble to divulge them to you. Why don't you do the same? You'd see that such an exercise can not only be instructive and stimulating but also amusing.

For there is enlightenment inherent in every embarrassing episode, and while labourers in the vineyard of culture tend to forget their successes quickly, the memory of a project that came to nothing stays in the mind for years, if not decades, with a quite compelling intensity. While triumphs hold no lessons for us, fiascos can extend our understanding in many ways. They give insight into the conditions of production, conventions and practices of the industries concerned and help the clueless novice to assess the snares, minefields and possibilities of shooting oneself in the foot that one must expect in that area. As well as that, flops have a therapeutic effect: they can if not cure then at least alleviate the vocational illnesses of authors such as loss of control or megalomania.

I for my part am quite happy to admit that there are few experiences to which I owe so much as to my flops; I even maintain that with the years they have become more and more dear to me.

Thus I would like to present to you a review of failed projects with which I have occupied myself more or less intensively. So far there has been no scientific assessment of the factors that can lead to a flop, nor a practicable classification that would have to take account of height of drop, mass, visibility and observer's position. Nor can this little collection lay claim to completeness: by the very amount of material it would contain, a complete book of samples would run the risk of wearying the reader.

Moreover there is probably a whole range of other projects that I have quite simply forgotten.

Here and there I will complement my account with all sorts of excerpts. Anyone who finds these interruptions distracting is welcome to simply skip over them. That should not present any difficulty, for those passages are clearly marked out typographically. Let the critics condemn them, others I hope will find them amusing.

It is the stage that has by far the best flops to offer. A book, even if the worst comes to the worst, can look forward to a lifespan of at least a few weeks before the lack of interest among its readers and critics has made itself sufficiently clear so that, after a series of scathing reviews it disappears without trace; an unsuccessful theatre production, on the other hand, gets the chop with a speed that recalls a well-oiled guillotine—you imagine you can hear the dull thud of the blade doing its job. That's why my theatrical flops are the most unforgettable and dearest to me.

I can understand authors who don't like looking back on their major or minor failures—it's well known that there's no justice in the arts. Even the most absolute beginner suspects that since time immemorial lies, intrigues and fiddles have been the order of the day in the arts. That is how the business works. To join in the equally familiar laments about that is evidence of a sensitive soul but won't get you anywhere. Instead of wasting time on such complaints it makes more sense to play the next card you have up your sleeve and, as it says in a 1793 pop song, 'Enjoy life since the lamp's still shining'.[1]

That shouldn't be all that difficult.

---

[1] From the poem 'Gesellschaftslied' written by J. M. Usteri in 1793 that was—and still is—popular as a song composed by H. G. Nägeli. [All notes in this volume are by the translator.]

My Failed Film Projects

My Failed Film Projects

It is well known that the film industry is the one that can boast the highest abortion rate. Its customs and practices are, as all involved will tell you, barbaric. That is probably connected with the fact that films are horrendously expensive. Anyone who has the misfortune to think in moving images must expect obstacles of which a poet or essayist has no idea because the production costs of their slim volumes are ten thousand times lower than those of a Hollywood film. Just as in the global art market, success in the cinema depends on a massive injection of capital. Money is the cocaine of both industries.

In the opening and closing credits of a feature film you can see the result of this injection—to a background of resounding music, the screen is teeming with the names of producers. The term is somewhat misleading, for strictly speaking these people mostly don't produce anything or invest their own money in the product. (People such as Bernd Eichinger or Nico Hofmann are the exceptions that prove the rule.) They really ought to be called brokers, who live off their commission.

Despite that, or perhaps because of that, they insist on informing the audience of their names right at the beginning in the biggest possible type size. In this there are no limits to their inventiveness for, along with the actual *Producer*, the names of the *Executive*, the *Associate*, the *Administrative*, the *Consulting* and the *Co-producer* appear on the screen. The main reason for the presence of these people is to procure the necessary money, administer the finances and supervise the staff. Thus they are concerning themselves with things that are much more important than the film itself, for they are constantly having to negotiate with investors, banks, insurance companies, distributors, TV broadcasters, ministries, unions and grant-awarding bodies. Only after them do we see—in a fiercely contested order and type size—the stars, the director, the cameraman and so on, right down to the lower regions of the credits where the screenwriter, the hairdresser, the script girl, the drivers and other lower ranks can be found.

Thus authors who, of their own free will get involved in this industry knowing the way it works, have only themselves to blame. As a rule, what they produce will end up in a drawer. Should it, against all expectations, be made into a film, they will hardly recognize their screenplay after all those years. If they employ a capable lawyer, they can at least see to it that they are compensated and their name withheld.

Jonas

My first 'cinema flop' was the result of mere chance. Someone must have told Dr Ottomar Domnick, the Stuttgart specialist for neurology and psychiatry, that there was a promising young man at South German Radio who enjoyed the reputation of being a 'nonconformist'. In those days, it must have been around 1954, that meant you were seen as a member of a kind of lodge—the concept of 'lateral thinking', that was to become so popular later on, hadn't yet been coined. It probably meant someone who had a high regard for the Bauhaus, the latest in abstract art, jazz and pieces of furniture such as the radio-gram—which later made it to the Museum of Modern Art as an iconic design. It was, moreover, one of the peculiarities of that tiny minority that they refused to accept the leftover vestiges of the Nazi regime.

Dr Domnick was well-known in Stuttgart as a member of this invisible order. He owned a private clinic; his clientele comprised the families of the local industrialists. He invested a large part of the proceeds in his collection of contemporary art, which he not only supplemented with lectures and books, in 1950 he also made a film entitled *New Art—New Vision*.

Ambitious and single-minded as he was, he wanted to show cinema audiences what he thought of the neo-Biedermeier[2] of the post-war reconstruction years as well. Between 1954 and 1956, he produced singlehandedly a feature film called *Jonas*, that was intended to be a kind of alternative to successful films with titles such as *Love, Dance and 1000 Hits* [*Liebe, Tanz und 1000 Schlager*] or *When the Evening Bells Ring* [*Wenn die Abendglocken läuten*]. He went about it in a rather haphazard way, filming without experience, without stars, without a studio and without a completed screenplay. Only when he'd finished shooting did it occur to him that the music of Duke Ellington wasn't enough to make it clear what he was trying to say with his film. To put it briefly, he rang me up and asked if I would be willing to provide a kind of soundtrack to go with his images.

Only an absolute beginner such as I was would have let themselves in for such a hopeless task. The film had already been edited and all that could be done was to sew it together with a kind of prose poem. Wet behind the ears as I was, I even

---

2 Refers to the early nineteenth-century Austrian and German art and culture—pertaining to the period between the end of the Napoleonic Wars and the 1848 Revolution—distinguished by its cosy, bourgeois character.

liked this extravagant procedure and, anyway, I could use the money Dr Domnick was offering.

The critics were delighted with *Jonas*. The 'experimental' film, more black than white, even won a federal film prize and a Bambi Award. Only the audience insisted on staying away. This reaction gives me the pleasure of installing *Jonas* in the place of honour in the list of my flops.

Traitors

I had better luck with a script that a German TV company com-
missioned from me about 40 years ago. The fee, though not lavish, was paid without hesitation, but it was never filmed. The
screenplay had the title *Traitors* and was set, if I remember
rightly, in a manor house in the Netherlands, among the political police in Amsterdam, somewhere in Kensington and in a
graveyard. The characters were: a professional South American
revolutionary; a Russian émigré; an American agent; an old
night-club singer and five gypsy children . . . And to top it all
there were also historical flashbacks involving the Czarist secret
police in the figure of the hard-boiled terrorist Evno Asev. He
was in fact a virtuoso at double-crossing.

Rather a lot all at once, the whole thing too complicated and,
of course, far too expensive! I had a great time working on it
and was not at all surprised when Herr Dr Rohrbach, at the time

the all-powerful head of drama at West German Broadcasting, quietly laid my melodrama to rest.

Here is the opening sequence of the screenplay:

Interior. The office of the political police in Amsterdam. At first, Ann Vanmeulen in the visitor's chair and the Inspector, in plain clothes, cannot be seen. The camera focuses down on the desktop and the Inspector's forearm.

INSPECTOR. Passport. Wrist watch. Some coins. Two hundred fifty English pounds in cash. Three capsules. (*He tosses the capsules onto the desk.*) That's all. It's not much. The autopsy gave no indication of a crime.

A mid-shot of Ann, from where the Inspector sees her.

ANN. As I can well imagine. The people who killed Manuel are not amateurs.

INSPECTOR. You call him Manuel, Mrs Vanmeulen. Please have a look at this passport.

ANN. Manuel was an acquaintance, but I know nothing about him.

INSPECTOR. I also have here a telex from Santo Domingo. Perhaps that will be of interest to you. 'Hasselblatt, Dr Carlos, alias Manuel Cuera, medical student. Wanted for bank robbery, extortion under threat of force. Political terrorist. Presumably living in France or Belgium at the moment.' And so on.

ANN. Of course . . . You and your colleagues over there . . . Thugs work together.

INSPECTOR. I believe you're deluding yourself. (*He gets up and looks out of the window.*) Admittedly I don't know much about Santo Domingo. I was only once in South America and that's quite a while ago now. I saw a hospital there, in Barranquilla. I imagine what it would be like if I'd been twenty-five and had studied medicine . . . The poverty's indescribable. Do you perhaps think I might have become a police doctor? The impossibility of getting anything done by legal means . . . A handful of brilliant friends . . . Che's ideas . . . The guerrilla unit . . . The group carry out their first operations, they're successful. They have to get money, they need guns. Do you really think I can't imagine that?

ANN. So you've summoned me here in order to explain Che Guevara's ideas. You of all people!

INSPECTOR. Yes. And then one day the organization's busted. An indiscretion, an agent provocateur, a spy. The whole group have to flee the country. So now they're far away from the action, in exile, somewhere in Europe. The less they can do, the more doctrinaire the leaders become. The result is the usual splits, suspicions and desperate gestures. Powerlessness can make people go out of their minds. I think I know how Manuel must have felt.

ANN. Oh, do stop it. That's all I needed—the political police full of understanding for the activist. Because he can't defend himself any more. Because he's dead you suddenly feel sympathetic towards him. You're a pig and a pig always lies. Even when he's telling the truth.

INSPECTOR. So you're not going to help us.

ANN. I've no idea how. Or why.

INSPECTOR (*sits down again*). Listen, Mrs Vanmeulen, you don't need to prove your political reliability here. We know who you are. (*He takes out an index card.*) Ann Vanmeulen, student, born 1946 in Loenen. June 1968 . . . Well, yes . . . November '72. Suspended sentence of three months for a public order offence, insulting an official, inciting to criminal acts.

ANN. If you're trying to blackmail me . . .

INSPECTOR. Perish the thought! We're just trying to find out who killed this man. Assuming someone did kill him.

ANN. At least that possibility has occurred to you.

INSPECTOR. My task is quite simple. For me the political background is of secondary importance. A foreigner comes to Holland—as a tourist, let's say. He's the victim of an unexplained accident. That's at least manslaughter with the driver failing to stop, isn't it?

ANN. If you're going to ignore the political background, then you can just forget the case.

INSPECTOR. I'll look into the matter. That's my duty. Everything we found on Manuel Cuera is on the table here. It's not much.

ANN. He had no possessions.

INSPECTOR. Do you know what these are?

Ann doesn't reply.

INSPECTOR. They're detonator caps that are used for plastic bombs.

ANN. Really?

INSPECTOR. And this here is the explosive charge. At least that's what it looks like. The odd thing is—I've had the content analysed—there's no explosive in it, it's just soft soap.

ANN. Why are you telling me all this?

INSPECTOR. So, you're not interested in the murderer being found. If there is one.

ANN. That's enough of your nonsense. You're never going to get hold of these people. Or do you intend to search the American Embassy?

INSPECTOR. You're accusing an American diplomat?

ANN. I'm not accusing anyone.

INSPECTOR. Right then. For the moment that's everything Mrs Vanmeulen.

ANN. When will the corpse be released?

INSPECTOR. It won't be released at all—we haven't been able to identify the next of kin.

ANN. The next of kin is me.

Etc., etc.

Lichtenberg

This excursion into television did not act as a lasting deterrent, for a few years later Peter Sehr lured me back with a film project that meant a lot to him. That wasn't difficult since we've been friends for a long time and I trust him, which I can't say of most of the other people in the film industry. Moreover, he suggested a subject that had always fascinated me. He wanted to make a film about Lichtenberg. This author is one of my household gods. I've always not only admired his *Waste Books* but also studied his letters. There is no more masterful Enlightenment-thinker in the German tradition and even in other literatures —the only one with whom he is at par, to my mind, is Diderot.

Peter Sehr was the ideal partner for that kind of enterprise because he is not only competent but also imaginative and persevering. Together we set about developing a fictitious story. In

August 1995, I presented my first outline. The following passages are taken from it:

The Subject

In this film science and love, two obsessions of the late eighteenth century, coalesce to make a fantastic drama. At that time physics was a new discipline, shrouded in mystery. A scholar from Germany, a genius, bachelor, cripple, writer and drinker, a protégé of the English king, is determined to solve the mystery of erotic attraction. For that he needs a guinea pig. He meets a 15-year-old flower girl and takes her into his house. The intimate research, which he undertakes using his innovative apparatus, both succeeds and fails at the same time. It is not the intrigues and attacks of a hostile environment that are decisive. The charm and vitality of the girl throw the scholar off course. He does make a great discovery—the power of love does indeed come from an unknown fluid—but death and life are stronger than his theory. When, after a few turbulent years, the young woman dies from some disease, they have both left their experiment behind: their love survived physics.

Main Characters

A genius—the disabled German physicist Georg Christoph Lichtenberg.

A young girl of great charm and intelligence who grew up in a slum—Dorothea Stechard.

A sympathetic king of England who is threatened by a psychosis
—George III.

A 16-year-old crown prince, who has started out on a career of
rake and schemer—the later King George IV of England.

King George IV's 30-year-old mistress, a demi-mondaine with
a taste for perversion—Mary 'Perdita' Robinson.

The Setting

London, a blossoming international metropolis during the
period of scientific discoveries.

Göttingen, a provincial small town in Germany with labyrinthine
alleyways—seat of the famous university.

The Action

London, the autumn of 1775. Lichtenberg visits the elegant shop
of the best instrument maker in the city. When he produces a letter from the king guaranteeing payment for any purchase, the
inventor lets him have the first model of his creation. It is a
gleaming brass electrostatic generator.

George III sends Lichtenberg an invitation to tea in Kew
Palace. He's interested in the new science—physics. A relaxed
atmosphere; the whole of the royal family is present. Suddenly
the King has a mysterious seizure. He speaks incoherently. The
Crown Prince makes a cheap joke about his father. The Queen
rebukes him and he stalks out, furious. The King recovers and

talks to his guest about the latest discoveries in the South Seas as if nothing had happened.

Later he goes for a walk in the park with Lichtenberg. He sees him as a person who knows what it's like to live with a disability.

An actress's boudoir with ghoulish furnishings. The prince tells Perdita about Lichtenberg's visit to Kew Palace. She has heard that the touch of a hunchback is a magic cure for impotence and suggests an experiment to the prince. She intends to seduce Lichtenberg. Then, at the decisive moment, her lover is to touch him. The prince sees in this plan a way of mocking his father, whose strait-laced family life he hates. Perdita is turned on at the idea of sleeping with a cripple.

They set a trap for Lichtenberg, who is oblivious to what is going on. His previous sexual experiences have been with waitresses and kitchen maids. He's easy meat for an experienced woman like Perdita. When the prince emerges from hiding, Lichtenberg realizes he's been tricked. He goes out of the house in disgust and leaves London post-haste.

The arrival of the electrostatic generator is a sensation in Göttingen. Professor Lichtenberg lives in an old house where he has set up a laboratory with a wide variety of instruments and devices. He has come to the conclusion that the energy of love is caused by an unknown fluid that shows similarities to animal electricity. He delivers a lecture on this, which eventually takes a bizarre turn: at the critical point, he falls off his high stool. The students' reaction is a mixture of curiosity, mockery and concern, causing him great anguish.

Lichtenberg recovers from depression, in time, and sets about conducting new experiments on electricity in the air. He constructs a kite in order to measure it. A crowd has gathered on the rampart in order to watch him perform the experiment. During his preparations he notices a young flower girl. He asks about her age and family background. She's called Dorothea Stechard. While the kite is still in air, he looks around for her. He fails to see the storm clouds gathering over the town. Lightning strikes the kite, which is earthed, and sends it tumbling down. The experiment is a failure.

The next day, the Professor goes to see Dorothea's parents. He would like to engage their daughter as a cleaner. The parents agree because Lichtenberg offers generous wages. Dorothea is to clean his scientific instruments. Secretly, however, he has a quite different plan. He wants to set about proving his discovery and the 15-year-old girl seems to be the ideal guinea pig. The two of them begin to observe and eavesdrop on each other. The secrecy creates an atmosphere of unexpressed desires. Lichtenberg teaches her to read and write. And, without direct physical contact, he succeeds in detecting traces of the erotic fluid by observing phenomena of fluorescence and resonance.

Just as the love between him and Dorothea is starting to spark, the scholar receives an invitation from the English king that is as good as a command—George III is also the ruler of Hanover. He has to set off for London immediately. George III makes a lodge in Kew Park available for him; and showers honours on the scientist. Lichtenberg becomes a member of the

Royal Society. At a reception, he is introduced to Omai, whom Forster brought back from Tahiti: the Polynesian can't understand why he isn't allowed to embrace a woman who's smiling at him simply because she's the daughter of the Lord Chancellor. His lack of inhibition makes a great impression of Lichtenberg.

Then there is a nocturnal conversation with the King in the Richmond observatory. George's personal physician is also present but stays in the background. Lichtenberg points at Venus and talks about the observations made during Cook's expedition to the Pacific. But the King has other things to worry about. Apart from the war with the American colonies, he is tormented by the fear of impotence and of a new psychotic attack. He is also perturbed about the Crown Prince. He even suspects his son is trying to kill him. He begs Lichtenberg to stay in London, offering him a position. But Lichtenberg has only one thing on his mind: his experiment and Dorothea, who is waiting for him in Göttingen. He gives an evasive reply. The King is hurt and commands him to stay.

The physician, whose prognosis for the King is not good —he's even wondering whether to have him declared incapable, has put his money on the Crown Prince, with whom he is in contact. He sees a danger for the latter's plans in Lichtenberg and tells the heir to the throne about the conversation in the observatory.

The following day, Lichtenberg is on his way to the theatre. Inside the carriage that arrives to pick him up, is a woman who offers herself in a downright unambiguous way. He's not going to be lured into a trap a second time. He threatens to throw the woman out of the carriage. The coachman turns to face him—it's the Prince. Instead of the woman, Lichtenberg is flung out into the street. He panics, steals the clothes of a gardener and flees. Under an assumed name he manages to board a ship which takes him to Hamburg.

The King proves generous. He forgives Lichtenberg, and has a new telescope and his clothes sent to Göttingen. Lichtenberg goes out in the streets in his new, elegant costume and shows off his new wigs to Dorothea. From now on he only speaks in English. He persuades his girlfriend to move in with him. He devotes all his efforts to build the machine for the great experiment. One night the decisive moment comes: as the two lovers come together, their union provides the clear proof of the existence of the fourth elemental force. The two of them are elated. However, there is a further question occupying Lichtenberg's mind: he is concerned about the durability of love. He secretly develops a storage device which, like a Leyden jar, will secure the power of love for the future; after all, he is 23 years older than his beloved.

He yields to the temptation to give a lecture on his great discovery to his students. Halfway through it he breaks off and disappears into his private quarters. Even though it is strictly forbidden for them to enter his residence, the students follow him and are surprised to find him with Dorothea inside a machine which measures and stores the fluid. The luminescence and coruscation are so bright that the voyeurs are left dazzled; and they soon flee.

The relationship between the lovers has changed. Dorothea, is not at all passive and submissive and has gained in self-confidence. The scientist is losing control over his experiment. It almost looks as if Dorothea in her own way is conducting an experiment with Lichtenberg. It comes to the point where she appears as hostess when the scientist invites his friends to his residence, which creates a scandal in the small town.

There is a confrontation at the end of the semester. The two of them attend the traditional graduation ball, to which all the town notables and the students from England are invited. A masked stranger asks Dorothea for a dance. Lichtenberg, who can't dance, watches the pair. The unknown man drags Dorothea with him out into the yard and tries to rape her. When she cries out for help three students rush out, corner the stranger, threaten him with drawn swords and tear off his mask. It's the Crown Prince. He's had to flee from England incognito because he'd stabbed and killed a rival in a brothel. The students, who recognize him, have to let him go. Lichtenberg is furious upon hearing this.

The town is abuzz with rumours about the weird experiments he carries out with Dorothea. People say that with his discovery he can bend any woman to his will. The suspicions arouse envy, fear and hearsay. Among the students, two groups emerge. Lichtenberg's opponents want to put an end to his endeavours, by force if necessary. The man behind them, who also funds them, is the stranger who has managed to maintain his incognito. He's the one who leads the crowd that gathers outside Lichtenberg's house one evening.

From the window, Lichtenberg and Dorothea see the approaching mob and their leader. Their intention is to destroy the mysterious machine. Let them go ahead, Dorothea says to her terrified friend. We don't need it any more. The couple hide in a wall cupboard. The machine is destroyed. But when the Prince sets about smashing up the large electromagnetic generator, he suffers an electric shock and falls to the ground. His followers think he's dead and flee.

It's a threatening situation for Lichtenberg and Dorothea. She tries to revive the Prince with mouth-to-mouth resuscitation. A doctor arrives; the Prince is saved and carried off on a stretcher. Furious at his humiliating situation he whispers to Dorothea, 'That's not the end of this. You'll see me again.'

The Prince returns to England. Lichtenberg, weary of the hostile atmosphere in Göttingen, moves with Dorothea into an enchanting summer-house outside Göttingen. The two of them have a new dream: flying. The news of lighter-than-air machines that can rise up off the ground comes from France. As a scientist, Lichtenberg wonders if there is perhaps a component of the atmosphere that is lighter than air. With the help of the few pieces of equipment he managed to save, he succeeds in isolating a small amount of hydrogen by electrolysis. He gets some transparent pigs' bladders from the abattoir and fills them with the gas. Dorothea is thrilled to see them float up to the ceiling.

Lichtenberg has also managed to save his electrophorus, his telescope and a few of his storage jars. Dorothea has no idea that they contain a supply of their love-energy.

Seven months later, Dorothea dies from tuberculosis. The Crown Prince appears to her in her feverish dreams and threatens her. At the same time, in her delirium, she sees Lichtenberg in bed with an unknown woman and that the Prince is mocking him.

Lichtenberg manages to snap her out of the nightmare. He opens the window and sends dozens of balloons floating up into the sky. We'll fly away like these, he tells her, describing the countries and continents they're drifting over. When Dorothea's breathing stops, he releases the last of the balloons in the air.

He only takes part in her funeral from a distance. The graveyard is close to the summer-house. Lichtenberg follows the route of her coffin from the roof, using his telescope. He then opens the green jars in which the fluid is stored. In an ecstasy of love, he goes into the large ground-floor room. There Dorothea is waiting for him on the sofa. She looks the way she was when he first met her. She doesn't say a word. Lichtenberg walks round her once then carefully sits down on the chair beside her. After a short while he says, 'I knew you'd come back.'

Four years later, Peter Sehr and I had a completed screenplay: *Lichtenberg; Or, The Fourth Power*. We also wrote a treatment outline in English for cinema and television for the Munich firm, Team Worx Produktion, since we suspected that our project would be unaffordable without a British partner. All this finally resulted in an option and screenplay contract; reading it was a pretty tedious task but at least it brought in a little bit of extra money. The project then set out on its protracted journey through the countless German bodies and presumably the odd broadcasting company as well. A lawyer was brought in and a state bank granted a subvention of a thousandth of the probable budget. After that there was the silence, usual in the industry, that has lasted until today. All the subventions, minimal as they were, have naturally long since been written off.

There is no question in this case of an ideal example of a total failure; the tireless Peter Sehr is far from consigning his favourite project to the grave. In the meantime, he has completed a number of films for the cinema but since he has a tenacity far beyond anything I possess, he will never give up his plan. He sometimes says that everything else he undertakes only serves as preparation for the great Fata Morgana he has in mind and which he can't abandon—*Lichtenberg: Mountain of Light*. I envy him, his patience and, despite my unwavering scepticism, I believe that one fine day he will be able to admire his *Lichtenberg* on the screen of the Arri Cinema—91 Türkenstrasse, 80799 Munich—which he runs.

Humboldt

I'm aware that the German film industry can manage perfectly well without me. I feel great satisfaction when it walks off with an international success which I can appreciate from the sidelines. Unfortunately, every now and then, I allow myself to get carried away when one of our important producers turns to me with a proposal. It doesn't happen very often, of course, but since I am of a forbearing nature I always go on the assumption that even in that industry there must be intelligent people who use their brains in their work.

One such man, who not only has a complicatedly intertwined empire of firms at his command but also understands the art of reading, asked me one day whether I thought a film about Alexander von Humboldt would appeal to a German as well as an international audience alike. Could I perhaps give him some practical help and advice? Yes, I said, I did know something about that exceptional man. I had, a few years previously, made an attempt to revive interest in that world-famous figure who was scarcely understood in his home country. The first step had been to bring his books out of the dusty libraries into the light of day. And, to general astonishment, that had succeeded.

Despite that I advised against such a bold project.

'It will be an expensive business,' I told him, 'one which, from what I think I know about your industry, will be beyond its means. What do you have in mind?'

'I've already spoken to those whose word is law about programming in the various TV organizations—if "organization" is the right word. They're excited. What we have in mind is a two-parter for prime-time viewing. At the same time, I'd like to get a cinema version off the ground.'

That was music to my ears but, as usual, I didn't believe a word of it. 'And how are you going to proceed?'—'I'd like to invite you to dinner with the major decision makers: an ARD[3] coordinator, a woman who's head of films with one of the channels—she's a friend of mine, I'm sure you know her name—and a director I'm confident is up to the task.'

It was a delightful evening and the cuisine cordon bleu. We were all agreed: it wasn't just 'doable', a start should be made right away.

---

3 A consortium of the regional public-service TV network in Germany; it runs *Das Erste* (The No. 1), the first national TV channel. The local stations produce programmes for the network as well as the regional channels.

The producer took me to one side and asked me to what extent I intended to be involved in the project. There was no question of me writing the screenplay, I said, that had to be left to people who are better qualified than me. Film might be a wonderful playground for project developers but even the most naive scribbler should be aware that a screenwriter is seen as a fifth wheel or, to be more precise, the conceited troublemaker you unfortunately can't entirely dispense with, but who suffers from the delusion that it is actually his film and then even complains about his meagre pay. Moreover, I said, I lacked the time to deal with the 13th version of a scenario. Even an extended treatment would be too much for me.

But I'd be happy to think it over. 'Let's just say I'll send you a kind of draft outline. About 30 pages. Then you can do what you like with it and I promise that once it's landed in your letter box you won't hear any more from me. I write and you pay— it's a simple deal. Should the film actually be made, I'll be delighted to have a look at the rough version without griping. If I should dislike the whole thing, I'll keep my mouth shut and forgo any credit that might be due. That way we can avoid any hassle.'

The producer didn't like that. 'But surely you'll be prepared to meet with the director and discuss things with him?'—'If you think so.'—'But you won't be available for promotion?'— 'Unfortunately not.'

The man kept his word to the extent that he sent me a voluminous contract that went into minute detail to ensure that all rights for all times and all countries in the world would go to his firm including those for so-called merchandizing, which presumably meant decorated cups, T-shirts and computer games. Also included were all commercial exploitations imaginable, not forgetting those that had not yet been invented. In the film industry that is called a buyout. I deleted a few absurd clauses, signed and set to work.

I liked it because I could give free rein to my imagination.

Initially my draft outline detailed the most important dramatic details a feature film would have to take into account:

Firstly: Alexander's biography is marked by such an extreme diversity of turning points, activities and directions that it would be hopeless to try and focus on them all. Substantial parts of Humboldt's career will have to be excluded, if his life is to be depicted in two episodes of a TV-programme.

I suggest, for example, skipping his stay on Cuba, in Mexico and the USA as well as his expedition to Russia. There can only be indirect reference to these very important events, for example, by mentioning them in the dialogue. (For example: 'My right arm's a nuisance, you can see how I have to support it while I'm writing. Tedious! A souvenir of my journey to Russia. It was damn gruelling! And what was the point of it all? 10,000 miles up hill and down dale and not for one moment did they allow me to pursue my research in peace . . . etc.)

And as for his famous journey to South America, the film will have to concentrate on a few episodes. On the other hand, the political background and motives, that played an important role in Alexander's life, must on no account be left out.

Secondly: In a certain way Alexander had no private life. He was an obsessive workaholic who, from his adolescent days to his death, hardly ever found time to sleep for more than four or five hours a day. However a film that ignored the emotional and sexual side of the hero's life would be bound to fail—no one in the audience would identify with a man who only lived for science. Major strands of the action should therefore be sought in Alexander's various intimate and emotionally charged friendships with men. The point is not how far he practised his homosexuality; it was always younger men who attracted him and with whom he established close ties. These relationships were asymmetrical in more than one sense: teacher–pupil; boss–subordinate; master–servant. That such combinations should lead to conflicts and disappointments was inevitable. The role of women must be emphasized as well: Alexander was a star; he was idolized; he was a much sought-after 'match' without it ever coming to a lasting liaison. The tragi-comic aspects of the consequent 'confusion of feelings' are abundant in dramatic material.

Since it is not to be a documentary film; it is both necessary and legitimate to invent whole scenes, concentrate several friendships in one figure and intensify the subsequent conflicts.

In order to deal with the above-mentioned diversity, the excess of action—intensified by Alexander's long life (as is well-known, he lived to be 93)—I suggest that the parts of his emotionally important friends—Graevenitz and Arago—as well as of his servant Seifert, should be performed by the same actor, who must be capable of playing the diverse roles, aged between 20 and 45. This can serve as a dramatic device to hold the film together and counter the greatest structural danger, namely, the loss of unity.

Thirdly: A further problem lies in the fact that the production depends to a great extent on the choice of locations. Above all this concerns the core of the action: the account of the great expedition. In this we can't always stick to the historically documented chronology.

Fourthly: Since it is to be a two-parter, that leaves us with the question of where the first part should end and the second begin. I suggest we should end Part One with his arrival in South America; with a conversation between Humboldt and an Indian in the dinghy in the roads off Cumana in Venezuela.

CHARACTERS

Alexander von Humboldt: All descriptions agree that he was very good looking, even in old age. Extremely concerned about his independence, persistent, with a manic enjoyment of work, very eloquent, occasionally malicious but also capable of self-irony;

incredibly enthusiastic, curious about things and with great powers of observation.

For his characterization we shall have to resort to *teichoscopy*: to the rumours spread by others. Disparaging comments: he considered himself omniscient, was vain, garrulous, a spend-thrift, arrogant, an atheist, unpatriotic, etc. Only very veiled references are to be made to his sexuality; otherwise all that's said is that he was repressed. People can't understand why he hates Berlin, visits his enemy in Paris, doesn't want a career in Prussia. That can be presented from the perspective of his brother Wilhelm and his wife Caroline.

In reality, Humboldt was an agnostic and politically a convinced, but not militant, republican. When it was a matter of pushing his plans through, he could display considerable tactical acumen. He was an outstanding diplomat—in that respect you could say he was no less cunning than Brecht. For all that, he never went so far as to deny his views. Privately he would express these very clearly, and neatly circumvent the censors.

Casting will be difficult. Since we are dealing with a span of 70 years, it's questionable whether we can manage with just *one* actor. If we did, he would have to be a virtuoso quick-change artist.

Wilhelm von Humboldt and His Wife, Caroline: From the very beginning Alexander's relationship with his older brother was a likely source of conflict. In order not to disturb the solidarity of the family, latent feelings such as rivalry, envy and jealousy were suppressed. They expressed their disapproval at the other's way of life. Arguments mostly broke out over politics.

Wilhelm was as highly gifted and energetic as Alexander but he saw himself as, above all, a servant of the state. Not an adventurer, more of a scholar than an empiricist. His wife Caroline, a lively Romantic, was always a bit ambivalent about Alexander. Perhaps she even liked Alexander as a man—better than her husband? That would explain her wavering between admiration and rejection.

Johann von Graevenitz: An invented figure. Synthesized from several young men who were close to Alexander. An officer from an impoverished noble family, very handsome, but of moderate intelligence. They meet in cramped conditions in provincial Franconia; Johann admires Alexander, who is superior to him in every respect. Mutual attraction is palpable, but the little lieutenant doesn't even dream of an affair. He has been engaged to a young girl from a similar background. However, the chronology of this story is sketchy, so the screenwriter will have to decide where it should be included at all.

Georg Forster: Alexander is first introduced to Forster when he's 20, while Forster is 36 and is already famous throughout Europe for his journey around the world with his father under the command of Captain Cook. For the first time Humboldt sees in him a role model he can accept without reservation.

Forster has taken service in Mainz as a librarian for the Elector—a 70-year-old archbishop and sovereign of the *ancien régime*. He is dissatisfied, sickly and in financial difficulties despite all his work and celebrity. His marriage to Therese Heyne, an unusually intelligent and self-assured woman, is crumbling. Politics in Germany is oppressive to him. But his influence on Humboldt was great and lasting. Nevertheless, Forster's wife rejects Alexander.

Aimé Bonpland: Alexander's already a famous man when he meets Aimé around 1798 in Paris. Aimé by contrast is 25 and naive, even though he's studied medicine and worked as a ship's doctor. His main professional interest, however, is botany. He is described as talented, courageous and skilful. Politically he, like Humboldt, is a convinced republican, but sexually he is very much inclined towards women.

The two lived in the same house: Humboldt on the *bel étage*, Bonpland in the attic. They developed a genuine friendship and even though, or rather, as always in such relationships, Alexander would surely have wished it could turn into something more; he didn't let it show. He supported Aimé and suggested he should accompany him on his great expedition as an associate scientist. In practice, however, he became a subordinate. For social and economic reasons, Bonpland was only granted the role of an assistant. On the other hand, during the journey Alexander was completely dependent on Bonpland, who never lost his good humour even under the most difficult conditions, while Humboldt suffered occasional bouts of depression. Humboldt disapproved of the way Aimé liked to amuse himself with native woman. The extreme conditions in the rainforest, the enforced intimacy and the unhygienic living conditions made everything fairly difficult. It is possible that Bonpland saved Humboldt's life at least once.

Their relationship becomes rather awkward after they return. Bonpland feels he was disregarded, that his contribution to the expedition didn't receive the recognition it deserves. He would go on strike and refuse to collaborate on Humboldt's book on their journey, which eventually led them to part ways. Embittered, Bonpland turned his back on Europe and came to a wretched end in South America.

Dominique François Arago: A close associate of Alexander's, whom he met in Paris in 1809, Arago was a brilliant scientist from Catalonia and 15 years younger than Humboldt. He was appointed director of the Paris observatory even when he was still young. Alexander admired him, considered him a prodigy and worked with him on his astronomical experiments. For a few years they saw each other almost daily.

Arago was married and extremely attached to his family, and would not reciprocate Alexander's passionate feelings. But even in his old age, Humboldt continued to write imploring letters to him from Berlin.

Seifert: Like Graevenitz, Seifert is also a fictitious figure— although a real-life model of the same name did actually exist at the time. Seifert, who has no first name, is Alexander's servant. He is first recruited at age 24, that is roughly 35 years younger than Humboldt. Another good-looking man, apparently the perfect manservant, devoted to his master, engaging, adroit and wily. Alexander addresses him by the familiar *du*, while Seifert sticks to the respectful form of address. Soon the two of them are completely dependent on each other. But this time the relationship comes to a bad, not to say, tragic end.

Later in Berlin, Alexander faces financial difficulties in his old age; he's spent his entire fortune on his researches. Seifert, a demonic character, exploits Humboldt's situation. He gradually takes over as master of the house. It comes to the point where his master is in debt to him and finds himself compelled in the course of time to write over his whole estate to him. This doesn't become known outside because Seifert maintains a proper facade. Their life together reveals the inner loneliness of the hero, who continued to work prolifically in his old age.

KEY SCENES
Part One

Credits and opening sequence. Close-ups of a scientific collection. Pictures of tropical plants. A chameleon in a cage. A parrot. Minerals. Shells. Insects. Soundtrack of noises from the rainforest: monkeys, birds, etc. Then a close-up of the famous painting showing Humboldt's laboratory in the jungle with his friend and assistant Bonpland. Maps are also to be seen, a celestial globe, a sextant and other measuring instruments. A medium shot reveals a study with many books and manuscripts. Finally, the master of the house, Alexander, now over 80, but busy and apparently fit. By the door his servant, Seifert, watching him.

Close-up of an illustration: Galvani's research on 'animal electricity' using frogs.

Next Scene: Alexander, around 23, is undertaking an experiment on himself. In a modest room somewhere in Franconia, he gets a helper to stick two blood-letting plasters on his back. They cause blisters that have to be cut open, then a silver coin is placed on the one, a piece of tin on the other. Strong electric shocks. Humboldt has dead frogs placed on his back. As soon as they make contact with the silver, the frogs twitch. Intense pain. His helper is concerned, doesn't know what to do. A doctor is called. He is left with two scars. Alexander sets about preparing his results for publication forthwith.

In 1789, he visits Forster in Mainz and confirms his intention to undertake a serious expedition. Forster takes him under his wing and invites him to accompany him on a journey to the Netherlands and France, which will eventually lead them to Revolutionary Paris. Humboldt is delighted and agrees. Therese is suspicious of the budding friendship. She disapproves of the planned journey. Alexander, she says, is 'sick and suffers from a nervous disorder'. She thinks he's a charlatan. And the fact that he's a baron tells against him in her eyes. Perhaps there's even a touch of jealousy in all this; he ignores her.

It would be too much to film the journey itself. That is particularly true of its conclusion in Paris. They get caught up in the frenzy on the first anniversary of the storming of the Bastille. But it has to be made clear that this episode has a decisive influence on Humboldt's political outlook. With Forster—who later met a

wretched end in Revolutionary Paris—he shared a critical attitude towards the authoritarian state; his repugnance towards the
power of the Church and the hope for a republican society. Perhaps a scene with a conversation in which all this is made clear
can be arranged.

Condemned to a career as a state official, Alexander decides
to choose mining—a field of great economic importance. The
newly acquired Prussian possessions in the Erzgebirge and the
Franconian Forest give him the opportunity to demonstrate his
organizational abilities and extend his knowledge of geology. He
works 14 hours a day, often goes into the pits, monitors operations and even increases the output of the neglected and run-
down mines fourfold. It's dangerous work. He experiments with
a miner's lamp to study the vegetation underground, faints and
is grievously injured during the process.

Here the camera can capture his hallucinations: part nightmares,
part dreams of dangerous, exotic journeys, possibly with an
erotic touch. Humboldt often appears delirious during the expedition—grappling with fits of fever or dizziness, for example, during the ascent of the volcano.

Barely recovered, he returns to work again. Humboldt designs a
novel breathing apparatus in order to protect the miners from
poisonous gas. At first they observe his energetic activity
bemused. Having never been properly trained, the miners are
ignorant. Alexander sets up the first further-education school for

them, which they attend rather hesitantly in the beginning, and then with increasing enthusiasm.

His success attracts the attention of officials in Berlin who are interested in reform. The minister sees to it that he is promoted and wants to make him director of Prussian mines.

Alexander, still in the civil service, falls in love with a 20-year-old lieutenant, Johann von Graevenitz. They live in the same house. Alexander slips scarcely veiled love-letters under his door. The torments of passion. Johann is very good-looking but appears naive and unsuspecting; he finds his friend's scientific interests disturbing. Amalia, his 15- or 16-year-old fiancée arrives; she's fascinated by Alexander. Humboldt, apparently in all innocence, suggests they set up house together. That would amount to a *ménage à trois*. To others it appears as if Alexander is courting her. Amalia is flattered but has a feeling there's something not quite right. Eventually, perhaps on a fateful journey to Italy, there's an outburst of jealousy and they break-up. Alexander can hardly get over the end of this friendship. It's the low point of his early years. His disappointment leaves its mark on him for a long time—he concludes: 'There's a lot to be said for loneliness.' He attempts suicide but is saved by chance. Work is his salvation; he takes refuge in his studies.

Wilhelm and Caroline are concerned—what's wrong with Alexander, what makes him evade their questions? There's 'a veil between us'. Caroline tries to marry him off; visits him with some of her friends. All in vain. Wilhelm says, 'It's unlikely he will ever be happy.'

Humboldt's mother dies in her little castle in Tegel—that gives us the opportunity for a flashback to his childhood: eerie shots from 'Castle Boredom', tussles with his older brother, the family fatherless, their mother cold and unapproachable but ambitious for her sons. Unrelenting lessons with their tutors Knuth and Campe. Alexander, mocked as 'our little apothecary' because he collects plants and insects, hides in the park at night and is caught. Secretly reads accounts of journeys around the world and longs to visit the tropics. His mother tells him what he is to do: have a career in the civil service.

Her death is a release for Alexander. The substantial inheritance makes him independent. That very evening, he attends the salon of Henriette Herz, a beautiful and cultured Jew. He announces that he is finally going to resign from the civil service, even though he is promised better opportunities by the minister. He reveals to his hostess, in confidence, that he is planning a great expedition overseas. That is impossible from Berlin—the city he detests for its provincial atmosphere. Only Paris comes to his mind—the scientific capital of Europe at the time, is worth considering. The government there has been funding expeditions for years in order to consolidate their colonial empire.

Alexander takes the collection of scientific instruments he has built up over the years with him. But they don't satisfy his demands. Since he now has the necessary means at his disposal, he can have the best items on the international market sent from England. We see the arrival of one such consignment—instruments for a man who makes a cult of precision: Hadley's sextant, theodolite, chrono-, hygro-, endio-, hypso-, baro and cyanometer, inclinatorium and so on. . .

Alexander, 28, arrives in Paris. The political situation is unfavourable, Napoleon is planning the invasion of Egypt. The government's plans for other expeditions, that Humboldt had hoped to participate in, are shelved. He comes to the decision that he has to go solo.

On the stairs of the Hotel Boston, where he lives, Alexander happens to meet one of his fellow tenants: Aimé Bonpland. Despite his pockmarks, the botanist, who is the same age as him, is good-looking. Humboldt needs an assistant and has the means to pay for his services. So he engages Aimé and decides spontaneously to set off for Spain because all his other plans have come to nothing. His brother Wilhelm, also in Paris, warns him, 'Are you crazy, risking your health and wealth, and your career?'

After all the difficulties, delays and disappointments, Humboldt has an incredible stroke of luck in Madrid. Through a diplomat acquaintance, he is received by the all-powerful Prime Minister Urquijo who, probably in order to advance his career, has become the Queen's lover and is, in practice, the one who rules the country. Carlos IV is impotent and feeble-minded. The royal meeting is arranged while the court is being held at the summer-house in Aranjuez. Alexander is well prepared; he has even learnt Spanish. He impresses Queen Maria Luisa and becomes the very first foreigner to be given a Spanish passport which allows him to travel around and explore the Spanish possessions in South

America. This was rather unusual because the Spanish were wary of espionage by other powers. The scenes with the intelligent minister, the nymphomaniac queen and the mentally deficient king will provide a lot of good material for the film. Alexander is exultant. Bonpland has to see that he will always play second fiddle in the great enterprise; he had thought things would be different.

Finally the two of them can embark on the *Pizarro*, a somewhat decrepit frigate, brimming with passengers and crew. An epidemic of typhus breaks out onboard. Soon the death-knell is ringing as two men die. Humboldt argues with the captain, who has no idea of hygiene. They decide to anchor at the nearest port, Cumaná on the coast of New Andalusia. The Spanish flag is hoisted and a shot fired from a cannon. During the night, while the ship is moored off, a dugout canoe arrives, steered by an Indian. Going against the captain, Alexander makes a spontaneous decision to go down into that boat and start a conversation with the Indian, who speaks Spanish. The conversation shows the clash between two cultures and states of mind. The Indian wonders what the odd stranger wants, since he's clearly not after plunder, which would have been his obvious assumption. Alexander tries to make his intentions clear to him—thus implicitly revealing his attitude to colonial rule. Once on land, Humboldt and Bonpland are carried away by the frenzy of discovery. 'We're running around like mad.' Frantically they gather together the plants and stones of the new continent. This can be shown as a rapid, kaleidoscopic montage.

Part Two

Guards appear outside the little port intending to capture the supposed English spy and his companion. It is not until he is in the Vice Governor's house that Alexander, by showing the king's letter, manages to allay the suspicion. Fulsome apologies. His men, he says, are unfortunately very uneducated. One of the best houses in the run-down small town is allocated to them. Servants are at Humboldt's disposal. He's taken to the slave market where prospective purchasers check the goods. He is outraged. His host tries to show him how essential slavery is to their society. Alexander buys off a few slaves from the dealers, and offers them money and freedom. The prisoners are as baffled as the officials accompanying Alexander.

The expedition sets off, even though the Vice Governor tries to detain them—the travellers were a welcome diversion for him. Humboldt engages Indian rowers and buys a large pirogue heavily laden with all the equipment. A journey by river through the rainforest: poisonous plants, predatory animals, swarms of insects by day; noises shrouded in the mist by night. Parrots and monkeys in the boat. Humboldt is busy making measurements and notes, while Bonpland gathers unknown plants.

They find electric eels in a pond while resting in the jungle. Alexander can't resist measuring them. Painful electric shocks, numbness, dwindling consciousness. (Analogous to the experiment with the frogs he undertook while still a young man.)

At a waterfall, the boat has to be dragged over land—a Fitzcarraldo quotation would be possible here. It is customary for Europeans and their luggage to be carried by Indians. Alexander refuses saying it somehow seems undignified to him. Bonpland raises his eyes heavenwards—such qualms are superfluous, he thinks. Once the pirogue capsizes. Alexander, who cannot swim, is saved by a naked, well-built Indian, who takes him in his arms.

They reach a remote mission station in the jungle that is run by a few old and completely disillusioned priests. Alexander witnesses an Indian being flogged, which leads to an argument with the oldest priest. Humboldt, he says, has no idea of the things he has to deal with there. No question of good, unspoilt savages. There was cruelty, cannibalism, apathy. Their attempts at conversion had failed, all he hoped for was to be able to return to Europe. Alexander disapproves of the mission. He tells the priests they didn't understand the Indians' way of life at all and, without realizing, were just doing their best to destroy it.

Alexander tosses and turns in the tent, restless, unable to sleep. He hears Bonpland disporting with an Indian woman nearby, and the following day takes him to task about it. An argument breaks out about sexual love. The reconciliation comes during a longish stay when a laboratory is set-up in the jungle. Both at work: measuring and gathering samples. The famous painting can be used for this, though it does improve on their situation and gives no hint of the discomfort the explorers have to put up with: parasites, Bonpland's bouts of malaria, the constant attacks of the insects.

In the summer of 1802, Humboldt arrives in Quito. He is preceded by his reputation, for the sleepy capital his visit is a sensation. A crowd of onlookers, schoolchildren and street urchins wait for him outside the city gates. He is taken in the archbishop's carriage to the house of a famous aged botanist. Bonpland, who is ill, follows in a less flamboyant vehicle.

(In fact, this scene was played out in Bogotà. However, the following scene is about the ascent of Chimborazo, Ecuador.)

It is important here to show the ambitious display of splendour by the colonial society as a contrast to the extreme rigours of the journey so far. A soirée in the Viceroy's summer palace is planned. The evening before the ladies of the town visit Alexander in his lodgings. He shows them the moon through his telescope —even that is something new there. When a striking beauty more or less throws herself at him, he notices that her coiffure is alive with lice. That doesn't seem to bother those present, and Humboldt takes the opportunity to show them the parasites through his microscope.

After the lavish dinner in the Viceroy's palace there is a ball. The music: first of all Haydn or Mozart on an out-of-tune piano, then a local band playing animalito, samba, Congo minuet. The women flock around Humboldt, a superb dancer, but no one takes any notice of Bonpland, who looks pale and feverish; he is jealous of Humboldt and soon takes his leave.

A vivacious lady tries to seduce Humboldt. He tells her that he is already married—to science. She merely laughs, pulling off his coat and shirt. His desperate resistance in bed. At the very last moment Alexander takes flight, finds a carriage and goes home without saying farewell. Perhaps when he returns to his quarters, he finds Bonpland has consoled himself by going to bed with the cook.

Then comes the ascent of Chimborazo, at that time considered the highest mountain in the world. Alexander, as always aware of the value of publicity, wants to hold the record whatever the cost. That, however, doesn't stop him from recording precise measurements and investigating the plant distribution (climate zones). He explains this very new approach to the hesitant Bonpland. The natives can't understand what he's after and think he's mad. No one there goes up the mountains where nothing grows. When at a particular point their bearers refuse to go any farther, the two of them have to carry the heavy load of instruments themselves. The religious fears of the Indians might play a part in this.

Their equipment is totally inadequate. Their boots are far too thin and let in the water; their European clothes are not up to the task. Altitude sickness, nose bleeds, nausea, vomiting, bleeding gums, vertigo. Despite all this Alexander calmly continues with his measurements. Bonpland starts to hate him; he's tempted to push him over a precipice. Shortly before they reach the summit, he forces him to turn back. But when Alexander stumbles at a dangerous place during the descent, he still rescues him.

No sooner had they returned than Alexander started writing a jubilant report for the world, including the Paris press. In it he doesn't mention that the expedition failed to reach the summit. He grumbles about the postal service: 'It's as if we were on the moon.' The collections have to be secured; the mail ships are endangered by the British blockade, by pirates, by incompetent captains.

In Cuzco, Humboldt studies the history of the Incas and their ruins. He meets a small group of Creole intellectuals who are not interested in archaeological questions but think it more important to overthrow Spanish rule: 'What are the dead to us? We have to think of the living.' Humboldt finds himself confronted with violent revolutionary rhetoric—terrorists in the underground, so to speak. The seeds of the struggle for independence are already present. He sympathizes with their goals but has doubts about their realism and distrusts their excited chatter.

He develops a plan to travel on, to Cuba, Mexico and North America. Bonpland has had enough and wants to return home. The continuation of his journey will not be shown in the film, just mentioned in the discussion in Paris during the following years.

Humboldt arrives in Paris in 1804. He is the hero of the hour, not least because the press has several times reported his death. Napoleon is at the height of his power. He sends for him. The audience is disagreeable. A famous dialogue: 'I've heard that you botanize.'—'Among other things.'—'My wife also occupies herself with that kind of thing,' he says, turning away and leaving Alexander standing there. Later his friends tell him that the Emperor regards him as an enemy alien and a Prussian spy.

Like Napoleon, Humboldt only has four hours sleep. He immediately starts working on his great report on his travels. A double life: on the one hand, he enjoys his appearances in the salons; on the other, he sticks to his plain lifestyle. In his study, he scribbles notes on his desk; when it's covered in pencil notes, he gets the joiner to plane the desktop smooth again. He receives illustrators, cartographers and publishers. He rejects anything that doesn't satisfy him. Money is not a concern. He pays for everything out of his own pocket.

Bonpland who, as always, is in his shadow, feels neglected and goes on strike. Humboldt is furious. They have a row. His faithful helper goes away angry.

A big party in Paris. There's dancing. Here, too, the women have their eyes on Humboldt. There is a tragi-comic end to a second seduction scene. It turns out that the woman is an agent in the service of the police. Partly on their orders, partly out of revenge for his rejection of her approaches, she denounces him. Alexander's servant is bribed, his apartment searched, his letters opened. This is connected with the political situation: Prussia is at war with France.

Wilhelm, who is in Paris as a diplomat, reproaches him for his 'lack of Germanness' and reviews his catalogue of sins: atheism, sympathy for the aggressor, throwing money away. Alexander's response is fierce criticism of conditions in Germany. Prussia itself is responsible for its collapse. He has better things to do, he says, and needs to think about his science. He will stay in Paris. Berlin, a dull place in a sandy waste, holds no interest for him.

1810–13: The victorious allies enter Paris. Napoleon has fled. Russians and Prussians occupy Paris. His brother Wilhelm is back there too. He is jubilant: 'You see! What did I tell you? You have to get back into favour with the King again. He wants to see you.' Friedrich Wilhelm III is interested in Alexander's reports. A rather shy, uncultured man opposed to any reform, he seems to be fascinated by the famous explorer, makes him splendid offers and demands that he show him Paris. Among other things, he wants to visit the observatory. Arago, a patriotic Frenchman and a republican, refuses to receive him, at which Alexander takes him to see his friend at the observatory disguised in civilian clothes. The visit passes off without a problem. Afterwards, Arago confesses with a smile that he recognized the King immediately but for Humboldt's sake he didn't want to risk causing a scandal.

1826: The most important volumes about his journeys are finished. Humboldt's fame throughout Europe is growing. He, however, is suffering from depression, he's restless and despondent. He's also worried about his 'horrific expenditure'. The Prussian king, who appointed him chamberlain years ago, wants him back in Berlin again and is becoming impatient. A letter arrives in which he commands Alexander to return. He has no choice but to obey. He arrives in Berlin: little houses, geese in the streets. A stark contrast to the cosmopolitan city of Paris.

1830: The King is bored and needs Humboldt to amuse him. Alexander finds the duty of attending court tedious, it gets in the way of his work, which he never gives up. He is working on his *Kosmos*, a universal natural history. Moreover, he wants to institute a fundamentally new policy on science: he promotes promising young researchers who visit him and ask for his support. His public lectures are immensely popular, they are attended not only by society ladies but by the 'people': students, artisans, innkeepers. Even the King and Queen are present.

This gives Alexander some protection against the camarilla of pietists and extreme reactionaries who, regarding him as a dangerous republican, atheist and cosmopolitan, do everything possible to get rid of him. This task has been taken over by Markus Niebuhr, an intriguing courtier who is incredibly ugly but highly intelligent, a member of the cabinet and court society. But as long as Humboldt enjoys the personal protection of the King, it is impossible to get rid of him. He is even appointed privy councillor and has the right to use the title of His Excellency.

1848: After the failed revolution Alexander is placed under police supervision, his apartment is watched and his extensive correspondence opened. The aim of this is to banish him from Prussia.

One of many evenings at the court in Potsdam: Humboldt speaks for a long time, a few of those present yawn or leave the table. The King tells a joke. Humboldt continues undeterred. Niebuhr stands up and cries, 'Humboldt is a bottomless know-all.'

Alexander replies, 'Niebuhr is a squinting cockroach.' The Queen intervenes and tries to calm things down.

The King seems increasingly disturbed and confused. There are rumours that this is the first sign of mental derangement. Niebuhr secretly makes fun of him. The Queen is concerned.

1849: Alexander is world-famous, but sad and lonely. It is only his work that keeps him going. He's 70 and employs a man-servant, Seifert, who is 24, good-looking, zealous and of perfect demeanour. Seifert reminds him of Graevenitz. When one of the countless foreign visitors appears, he is the one who decides whether 'His Excellency is receiving visitors'; he protects and cares for Alexander.

When a geographer tells Humboldt that Chimborazo is by no means the highest mountain in the world, that others have explored higher peaks in the Himalayas, Alexander is annoyed at losing the record of which he is prouder than of all his other achievements. He changes the topic and shows his visitor the treasures of his study—a live chameleon that he feeds in a cage, a parrot, etc.

Another visitor is Prince Regent Wilhelm who is looking for advice and tells him in confidence that his brother, the King, is close to a mental breakdown and will probably soon not be in a state to rule. A conversation about the unrest at court, the necessity of secrecy, the intrigues. Alexander gets on very well with the prince regent; at the same time that protects him against his enemies, who continue to regard him as an enemy of the state and would most like to have him expelled from the country.

Unnoticed by the outside world, Alexander is becoming increasingly dependent on Seifert. He's in financial difficulties and has debts with his servant, who is possibly in liaison with a usurer and is slowly getting the upper hand. Alexander lets him have control over his expenditure. (In contrast to the case with Bonpland the master-and-servant relationship has been turned upside down.) Alexander can't refuse him anything. He makes a will in which he leaves everything to Seifert.

In 1857, Alexander suffers a heart attack and is bedridden; still he works day and night on the fifth volume of *Kosmos*, which he will not live to complete. On 2 March 1859, he takes a break. On 17 April, Seifert delivers the manuscript to the publisher. Two days later, Alexander takes to his bed with a fever. Prince Regent Wilhelm, the brother of King Friedrich Wilhelm IV and later Emperor Wilhelm I, visits him when his life is nearing its end. Humboldt dies with the prince regent sitting at his bedside. (In actual fact the visit came a few days before Humboldt's death.)

Alexander is feverish and delirious. Perhaps he could pick up his last notes off the desk, no longer able to decipher them. The Prince is at a loss; he talks to him but can't understand his incoherent ramblings—a stream of memories and hallucinations. A montage of moments from the film, but in a dream-distorted form. His young friends also appear in them—everything he's been through in his life but also things he didn't manage to do.

Then he stops answering his visitor's questions. The film ends with the dream sequence.

I naturally assumed that most of these ideas would go straight into the waste-paper basket but that was all part of the charm of the enterprise.

Then, as I had foreseen, there followed that longish silence which seemed familiar. Once, in a cafe in Munich, I met up with the director who had originally been selected, a man of talent who was full of enthusiasm about Humboldt and especially keen on doing the ascent of Chimborazo. Unfortunately, it soon became clear that he was so busy that there was no chance of him finding the time for our large-scale project. That meant that the producer had to start searching again, a problem which, as I was forced to realize, was not rare in that industry. A little later I heard rumours of distant murmurs from the funding bodies. In the meantime, Daniel Kehlmann had published his novel, *Measuring the World*, which was a well-deserved worldwide success. In that book an Alexander von Humboldt came to light who was unknown to me but had many fine features. That had clearly come to the notice of a rival TV company and now the swords were out to see who would win the spoils; for it was unthinkable that our public-service broadcaster would take on two gigantic projects about poor old Humboldt: there was simply no question of splashing out the limited TV-licence fees on something like that. With all due respect to the great explorer, something that might just be acceptable in the case of football was in his case quite understandably unthinkable.

Did I laugh up my sleeve? I did not, but the fact that from the very beginning I had seen this end (*not with a bang but a whimper*) coming was at least some consolation. Many months later, and not without a certain hesitation, the agreed fee appeared in my bank account. From that I deduce that even in the film industry there are clearly honest people.

Hammerstein

It is from the most recent lucky dip at one of the firms that I'm going to take an example of the coexistence of lively interest and modest reserve. In 2008, and after a gestation period of 50 years, I finished a book on General Kurt von Hammerstein-Equord and his uncommon family. This book, of which it is impossible to say whether it is a piece of research, a biography or a novel, had a surprisingly positive reception. Oddly enough, it even appeared in one of those notable lists the book trade believes in. This minor media shock must have woken one or the other film producer out of his siesta.

If I remember rightly, no less than four or five of these great luminaries expressed interest in the subject. One of them, of whom it was said that without him nothing worked but with him everything did, even granted me an audience in a noisy bistro on Leopoldstrasse. I was impressed when he confided a few details of his life to me. His experiences, he said, had given him an understanding of the vicissitudes which my general had had to deal with, so that his interest in his fate was not just professional but also very personal. It was essential, he said in conclusion, that my book should be made into a film. He would see to it.

Other more cautious feelers from less high-powered CEOs followed. Many a cup of coffee was drunk over these deliberations. None of the interested parties lacked enthusiasm. In the background there even seemed to have been negotiations with the publisher over the film rights, over certain option contracts and stipulations. The mire in which these conversations got bogged down is like a swamp that has swallowed up Hammerstein and his family even to this day.

Josephine and Me

As a footnote to this delicate failure, I would just like to mention that recently a new proposal has appeared on the horizon, only this time it was not one of the greater or lesser moguls of the industry to whom it has occurred but two well-known authors from the stage, film and TV, who could look back on a series of famous films. They didn't simply 'produce'—that is, administer, manage and market—their own works, but shot them themselves. For that reason, they lacked the necessary funds. Still, it cheered me up that they'd asked me.

All this concerned a story I published in 2006. *Josephine and Me*. To call it a flop would be going too far, for even though most reviewers didn't like it, it was translated a lot and even had some readers in Germany. But who can say how surprised I was when a top German director asked me whether I would mind his putting my story on screen as a full-length film. It was none other than Werner Schroeter. And he had earmarked as producer, his friend Wim Wenders, a genuine artist, that is.

We met for the one and only time for lunch in the tomb-like cafe of the Hotel Kempinski on the Kurfürstendamm in Berlin: Schroeter, his wife, my friend Ingrid Caven, who was to take the lead and me. Werner was a quiet, impressive man who looked fragile and was a good listener. As always, he knew exactly what he wanted. You could tell that he was in poor health. He ate little and only drank a glass of water. Despite that he seemed not only composed but confident, not to say, cheerful. We were all stimulated by his spirit and we felt our project was getting under way. We will not see Werner Schroeter again, for he died only three months after the meeting.

My Failed Operatic Projects

My Failed Operatic Projects

Operas are wonderful. Like the people who work on them, they're mostly both crazy and expensive. I can't remember how often I've turned my hand to this art, diffidently and with a total lack of success. I once wrote a play, *The Philosopher and Death*, based on the great Chinese author Lu Xun. At that time the famous Korean composer, Yun I-sang, was living in Berlin. It was no mere chance that he was passionately interested in Lu Xun for, like him, he was familiar with political oppression from personal experience. In 1967, he had been abducted by the South Korean secret police, tortured and, in a show trial, sentenced to lifelong imprisonment for treason. A wave of international protest led to him being released after two years. He found refuge in Berlin and took German citizenship. He told me he intended to compose a chamber opera based on my short play. Nothing came of it, for Yun I-sang died before he could get round to it.

I had more luck when, together with my close friend Irene Dische, I wrote a libretto for the Finnish composer Aulis Sallinnen. *The Palace* was actually premiered in Savonlinna in 1995; there is even said to be a DVD of the opera.

Even when we went one step further and tried to fix Mozart's wonderful 'Lyrical Drama in German', *Zaide*, which in the eyes of the experts was tantamount to a crime, but the little Hebbel Theatre in Berlin was prepared to risk a performance. When Mozart wrote that magnificent music he had no money to pay a librettist, so he had to make do with the services of a Salzburg court trumpeter, whose text guaranteed that it wouldn't work on the stage. Even today no one has yet succeeded in turning the absurd plot into something performable; usually people make do with concert performances or records.

The task as we saw it was to create a libretto that fitted Mozart's score down to the very last note and syllable. His *Zaide* is a so-called Turkish opera, a genre that was very popular in Europe in the last quarter of the eighteenth century. Its greatest triumph was Mozart's immortal *Il Seraglio*, performed a few years after his flop with *Zaide*.

Our solution was to devise a plot from the present-day Near East; we turned the sultan into a guerrilla leader and the kidnapped Christian woman into the spoilt daughter of a billionaire. This risky operation gave not only us but also the audience a lot of fun, and although it had little appeal for the guardians of Mozart's legacy, I feel I am not in a position, unlike the following cases, to include it in the list of my failed projects.

La Cubana

After every horrendous flop the eternal question always arises: 'Who is to blame?' It is asked out loud or behind people's backs, in the foyer, in the dressing rooms, in the artistic director's office, in the newspapers. All those involved are possible culprits, from the conductor right down to last supernumerary.

That was the situation after a first performance in the Theater am Gärtnerplatz in Munich on 25 May 1975. What had been put on was *La Cubana oder ein Leben für die Kunst* (La Cubana; Or, A Life for Art), a vaudeville in five scenes. The central character was a real person, Amalia Vorg, known as Rachel, a famous music-hall star from Havana's golden and filthy years between 1906 and 1934; the Cuban writer Miguel Barnet had written her biography. The play was set in a framework showing the aftermath of the revolution one year on from the triumph of Fidel Castro.

The music for this was composed by Hans Werner Henze, who was a friend of Barnet, as I was. As the librettist I am not qualified to judge, but I would still like to risk one comment: it cannot have been due to the music that the evening turned into a disaster. Henze, intoxicated by the charm of Cuban music, which he knows very well, broke all the rules which, at the time, were regarded as *de rigueur* for any serious composer, and still are today, even if they are no longer adhered to so rigorously. The composer took the liberty of writing songs that were not only singable but very catchy: numbers for buskers, for a circus, for a poncy palm-court orchestra and for the funeral march of a military band. He deployed two bombardons, a tenor banjo, a voodoo drum, a marimbula, a pianola, steel drums from Trinidad, car horns and pot lids to charm the listener's ear—all things that were supposed to be taboo for so-called serious music.

I have no real answer as to why the productions was a total disaster, despite all that, but perhaps something Henze himself told me will help explain it. On a flight home from an engagement in New York there was a young man sitting beside him with whom he got into conversation and whom he liked. It turned out that he was an actor and director working in Chicago and New York. Henze couldn't exactly remember what he was called. Something beginning with M . . . Markovicz? Moskwitsch? Or even Malkovitch? 'Why don't you send me a recording of your latest work?' he asked the young man and, indeed, shortly afterwards a videotape arrived in Marino that demonstrated the young man's talent. Henze, who was always very keen to encourage gifted younger colleagues, was so taken with him that he demanded that German theatres who were eager to put on a first performance of his work should engage that director. The Theater am Gärtnerplatz agreed to this condition. The conductor, the stage designer and the singers were all signed up, the date of the premiere settled, and the rehearsals began.

Two weeks before the first performance Hans Werner Henze arrived in Munich to realize that the theatre had got the wrong name. It was an understandable mistake. While no one had ever heard of the young American, Imo Moszkowicz was an established name. This charming man returned to Germany after the war, even though he had been deported to Auschwitz with his family in 1942, and had a remarkable career in this country. He could look back on over 200 successful TV-films such as *Der Ritter vom Mirakel* [after Lope da Vega's *El caballero del milagro*] and the children's series, *Meister Eder und sein Pumuckl*. The seasoned director treated *La Cubana* with such respect that he refused to cut anything from the all-too-profuse text and score. The conductor and the singers were determined to make the most of the famous composer's every note which, as it seemed to me, slowed down the pace of the production. Not that I can claim any kind of expertise in musical matters, but I do remember that it was so warm in my box that I had difficulty keeping my eyes open and was asleep before the interval. Even the feeble applause failed to wake me. Later I heard that the same had happened to part of the audience, though most of them did hold out until the end of the performance.

The inevitable first-night party was held in a bare room with small tables. The mood was remarkably subdued and most of those present soon left, slipping out past us with a 'We'll give you a call'. Not long afterwards *La Cubana* had disappeared from the theatre's repertoire.

To round off this tragi-comic story, I'd like to quote the 'Old Reviewer's Song' from my libretto:

> Yes, I discovered her, fifty years ago,
> I did, the great Rachel, when she was just a little hussy,
> I did, for a few cents and a comp ticket,
> the conscience of the Cuban stage.
> Today, of course, people say it wasn't real art.
> Easily said, afterwards, when no one fancies
> Rachel any more. But back then! Your mouth watering!
> As a critic I tell you, back then and today,
> if something makes your mouth water,
> then I don't care what people say, it's art
> and nothing else.

Politbüro

In 1991 everything suddenly disappeared: the Soviet Union, the Warsaw Pact, the Iron Curtain. And what happened to the Politburo? No one mentioned that terrifying word any more. What had actually become of the members of that highest of all committees?

That was something we—Irene Dische and I—were wondering one day and we came to the conclusion that it was time to visit those gentlemen and put together a memorial to them in the form of an opera buffa.

Our libretto is set in the capital of an unnamed east- or central-European country and the following are the main characters:

The Chairman, a nameless apparatchik; Comrade Hollo, his deputy, who is looked on as a reformer; General Matschikowski, the former defence minister; Comrade Schlitz, ex-head of State

Security; Comrade Taufer, ideologist and specialist in propaganda; and Comrade Gröger, a long-time associate. These gentlemen, who are all over 75, are not in the best of health. One has bladder problems, another can't manage without his insulin and a third is badly affected by cirrhosis of the liver.

The following therefore appear to give them a helping hand where necessary: a Senior Consultant with his assistants—the Strong Nurse and the Kind Nurse as well as a couple of hefty Male Nurses. The chorus of their Faithful Wives can be heard offstage now and then, vainly asking to be allowed in.

The stage setting is a six-person hospital ward with iron-framed beds and old-fashioned, white-painted metal furniture. The room looks dilapidated. The only contact with the outside world is through the one door into the corridor. A small, barred window high up in the wall is covered with blankets. The atmosphere is that of a run-down old-folks' home. It's also clear that none of the inmates may leave the hospital.

The action begins with the wake-up bell, at which the old men sing one of Lenin's favourite songs in their croaky voices. Later the boss convenes a conspiratorial session of the Politburo. They all push their iron bedside tables together to form one long, wobbly conference table and gather around for a review of the situation, which comes out as a liturgical antiphon. Furious disagreements as to the correct party line lead to reprimands, confused bickering and threats of expulsion.

When Strong Nurse announces the Doctor is about to do his round, order is hastily restored, the inmates, as well as their tables, return to their beds. The mood following the Doctor's diagnoses is depressed and the jokes from the days of the Great Purge do little to brighten it up.

Suddenly a Women's Chorus can be heard from backstage; *sostenuto* chanting in the style of solemn funeral marches. It is the Faithful Wives lamenting events in the outside world, but they are not allowed in. One of the following scenes shows how the Politburo reacts:

Two orderlies lug in a huge TV. It is veneered and has wide, gold ribbons tied around it. The patients stand up, overcome by the sight.

KIND NURSE. A present for you gentlemen, for the anniversary of the Revolution. Now guess who it's from.

VARIOUS CRIES FROM THE PATIENTS. Our provincial comrades!— My special units.—-North Korea.—So the illegal network is still active after all!

KIND NURSE. There, you see. You don't deserve people caring for you, you old sillies. It's your wives bringing you presents because they're always thinking of you.

Astonished, the inmates gather around the TV-set. The Chairman switches it on. The audience can't see the screen, but the sound plays an important role. It's very poor. It should also be manipulated musically (filter). At first there are commercials with a background of pop music that can be heard: an airline extolling travel to the South Seas; a bank promising immense profits from its shares.

CHAIRMAN. Just look at that! The anniversary of the Revolution and no parades, no speeches, no rockets. That's decadence for you. The class enemy has won. (*He switches over to another channel. Now it's some porn. Corresponding noises. The men move closer to the screen.*)

Disgusting! Switch it off at once.

MATSCHIKOWSKI. Oh, leave it on.

HOLLO. You have to keep your eye on the ideological enemy.

SCHLITZ. Oh, don't make such a fuss. You've watched that at home every day.

Gong. The Senior Consultant comes rushing in followed by the Strong Nurse.

SENIOR CONSULTANT. Where has this television come from? (*Muttering.*)

KIND NURSE. Oh, Professor, let them have this pleasure for the few days left to them.

MATSCHIKOWSKI. What do you mean, few days left to them?

SENIOR CONSULTANT. From a medical point of view any excitement is to be avoided.

STRONG NURSE. The television set must be removed.

CHAIRMAN. No way!

Strong Nurse calls on the orderlies for assistance. There's a tussle over the TV. Suddenly the screen goes black, the sound breaks off abruptly.

CHAIRMAN. What's going on?

SCHLITZ. Interference.

HOLLO. Perhaps there's a power cut.

CHAIRMAN. Nonsense. (*To the orderlies.*) Take your filthy hands off my television.

Sound is suddenly restored. Solemn music.

ANNOUNCER. Your attention, please. This is a special announcement for all channels. Under Comrade Zander, general and member of the Supreme Security Council, a committee to rescue the country has been formed and is taking over the government with immediate effect. A state of emergency has been declared for the whole country. Troublemakers and plunderers will be shot on sight. All citizens should remain calm. There will be a strict curfew from nine o'clock in the evening.

Distant shots and detonations can be heard from the TV. Hollo starts clapping.

CHAIRMAN. Stop that! These are nothing but carpetbaggers. It's a catastrophe!

TAUFER. Putschists.

MATSCHIKOWSKI. Zander of all people! That stupid idiot! He doesn't even have control over his troops.

SCHLITZ. They've got in before us.

MATSCHIKOWSKI. The wrong people.

TAUFER. Behind our backs.

CHAIRMAN. A bunch of amateurs.

HOLLO. Well at least . . .

CHAIRMAN. At least what?

HOLLO. At least they've made a start.

SCHLITZ. So what?

Babble of voices on the TV. Shots heard. Then military marches again. Interference.

CHAIRMAN (*to the Consultant and the Strong Nurse*). Don't just stand around here. Haven't you realized what's happening? The tide has turned. (*Bellows.*) I will call you all to account! Now get out! And make it quick!

Senior Consultant, Nurses and Orderlies leave, frightened. Interval.

Kind Nurse enters with a trolley. She's bringing dinner. Stew in metal bowls. Sound of spoons in the darkness, perhaps backed up with percussion. The marches on the TV break-off abruptly. Upon hearing the first words from the announcer, they all gather around the TV-set.

VOICE OF THE PRESIDENT. Fellow citizens, we can all breathe a sigh of relief. The criminal putschists have been disarmed, constitutional order has been restored. The ringleaders have been arrested. They will be put on trial as soon as possible. I thank our brave soldiers who have inflicted the defeat they deserve on those men who are still living in the past. I thank you all for keeping calm. May our great country continue to enjoy peace, democracy and prosperity. (*An invented national anthem is played.*)

CHAIRMAN. Switch off. Switch off at once. Those losers!

MATSCHIKOWSKI. Loads of shit.

SCHLITZ. I knew right away.

HOLLO. So that's it, then?

TAUFER. So you say, but I'm telling you—the day will come . . .

CHAIRMAN. That's for sure.

HOLLO. But without us.

CHAIRMAN. End of discussion. Off to bed all of you.

Götterdämmerung. The members of the Politburo stumble, stagger crawl into their beds.

CHAIRMAN. A song. 'In darkest dungeon . . .' (*He gives the note, feeble singing. Some confuse the verses. The tune sounds very odd.*)

CHOIR. In darkest dungeon tortured
By the enemy's whips and knives,
In the fight for our nation's future
We gave our blood, our lives.
Through days of care and sorrow
Our country's love we invoked.
They couldn't break our spirit,
It was our hearts they broke.

We trust, yes this we know:
The future will be ours.
We know that freedom soon
Will smash the dungeon's power.

Lights dim slowly. The end.

It was child's play for Irene, who can not only play any piano arrangement at sight but also knows all the important conductors, to obtain an audience with the director of the Deutsche Oper in Berlin. He was a gracious ruler who must actually have read our libretto for, after lengthy consideration, a contract arrived between 'the *Land* of Berlin, represented by Deutsche Oper Berlin, Richard-Wagner-Str. 10, 10585 Berlin' and the two authors, together with an 'Addendum to §2(3): it is possible that in the opera certain battle songs from the communist tradition will be quoted. In that case any payment for minor rights arising will fall to the Deutsche Oper.' And not only that. There was even money available, and for the composer as well, and the one proposed was none other than Wolfgang Rihm. Once more we seemed to have had the ideal solution.

For Rihm was not only famous when we met him, he turned out to be charming and extremely witty. I was pleasantly surprised, for his music had always struck me as rather loud and Teutonic and I was wondering whether he was the right man for our libretto, with its mixture of farce and endgame, Feydeau and Beckett. Such misgivings would have vanished on the spot had our composer not just suffered a great misfortune. His mother had died and Rihm fell into a long-lasting depression.

So the years passed. Our director took his well-deserved pension and there was no word from his successor.

After seven years we took out our faded contract and found the following:

If the Deutsche Oper does not take up its exclusive right to the first production of the opera within five years after the beginning of the scheduled season, Herr Enzensberger will have the right, with the agreement of Frau Dische, to reassert their exclusive right to the first production.

'I can understand your disappointment,' the new director said in his letter to us, 'that we cannot use your libretto now during my term in office either. But you must understand that I have of course extensive plans of my own in that direction.'

So it's no wonder that since then no more has been heard of *Politbüro*, any more than of the Politburo. Just like its main characters it has quietly passed away unnoticed.

Operette morali

The whole business is a bit sluggish, a bit tedious. It's a long time since Pierre Boulez wanted to set fire to the opera houses. My friend, Irene Dische, and I don't think that's necessary. It would perhaps be enough just to liven things up a bit. We've nothing against the *Magic Flute*, quite the contrary, and when the older stars from Budapest go on tour with *The Land of Smiles* or *Countess Maritza* we're quite moved. Like most other lovers of musical theatre, however, to the indignation of the music critics we avoid the shriller offerings of the neo-neo-avant-garde. Are there not some simple ways of reviving the art that's rather stuck in the mud?

For example, by trying out before one of the eternal reruns of *La Bohème*, something with a few singers who aren't involved in the current production: an *hors d'oeuvre*, an *amuse-oreille* or a curtain-raiser in the foyer before the performance—a few mini-operas by new composers lasting 10 or 12 minutes and intended for one-off consumption, the way you don't read the same number of a news magazine at breakfast every Monday morning. It wouldn't be particularly costly and might even arouse the interest of some people who know the repertoire off by heart.

So we set about concocting—on our own account, of course —a few short libretti under the title *Operette morali*, with the original meaning of the diminutive: 'pocket-sized operas'. We were, moreover, bold enough to hope that none of the many senior or assistant directors would have heard of Giacomo Leopardi, from whom we'd borrowed our title.

Since Irene knows her way around several of the leading opera houses, she informed this or that person of what we had in mind. 'A brilliant idea,' was the response, 'ideal for the next season.' It soon turned out, however, that our suggestions would have led to unacceptable disruption of the organization of the opera house. It was impossible to find out where this objection came from: the casting office, the head of administration, the employees' committee or the janitor. There was no mistaking the silence that followed. However, we still find some of our divertimenti amusing, even though since then other topics have dominated the talk shows, we don't want to withhold this collection from our esteemed readers. Which of us wrote which scene we can no longer say for certain ourselves; we are, as the lawyers say, jointly and severally liable and refuse to allow ourselves to be disjoined.

I. Possibly Leading to LTR

CHARACTERS
Karl-Otto Löblein (tenor)
Brigitte Kühl (alto)
Cafe personnel

Bachelor flat, Löblein.

KARL-OTTO LÖBLEIN (*on the telephone, singing*). Mature man, loving and intelligent, physically active, reliable, Taurus. (*Speaks*) Yes, Taurus, for God's sake. That's what I said. (*Sings*) Early retirement, no dependent children . . . (*Speaks*) No, delete that. What? No, not the children, the early retirement. (*Sings*) With both feet firmly on the ground, seeks straightforward, faithful woman with a natural aura for a future together. (*Speaks*) Only serious replies etc., etc.—How much is that?—No, no line spaces, single column. Yes, 'Mature man' in bold please.

A cafe. Two tables well away from each other. On the left Karl-Otto Löblein with a bouquet, on the right Brigitte Kühl with a pocket mirror and lipstick. Quiet pop music from the loudspeaker: 'Schenk mir doch ein kleines bißchen Liebe'—words by Bolten-Baeckers, music by Paul Lincke, 1904. Löblein is looking around, puzzled, but Brigitte doesn't give him a sign.

BRIGITTE (*sings along quietly*). Won't you give me just a little bit of love, love,
Come on, don't be so hard on me.

That's what I've been dreaming of, of,
Why won't you listen to my plea . . .

(Another pop song could be used instead. 'Nur die Liebe läßt uns leben'—words by Joachim Rein, music by Joachim Haider, 1971:

Only love makes life worth living
Days of brightly shining sun,
Days of joy and rapture giving.
Only lovers
Will never be alone.)

Löblein hums along. They exchange glances. Löblein gets up hesitantly, goes over to Brigitte and hands her his bouquet.

LÖBLEIN. May I? Löblein, Karl-Otto Löblein.

BRIGITTE. Brigitte Kühl, Kühl as in hot. Please take a seat.

LÖBLEIN. Pleased to meet you. May I call you Brigitte?

BRIGITTE. May I call you Karl-Otto?

LÖBLEIN. Of course.

BRIGITTE *(sings)*. Tell me what you dream about.

LÖBLEIN. Tell me what you dream about.

BRIGITTE *(sings)*. A cosy home.

LÖBLEIN *(sings)*. A woman to spend my life with.

BRIGITTE *(sings)*. A man of sensitivity.

LÖBLEIN *(sings)*. Security.

BRIGITTE *(sings)*. A happy home.

BOTH *(sing)*. Togetherness. *(They shout.)* And how do you see that?

The following duet is sung alternately.

LÖBLEIN. A compact oscillating sander with blowing action. Suction head up to 12 cm. Slip clutch. Power drive with maximum thrust. DIY drill stand.

BRIGITTE. Paradise duvet with extra natural-fibre filling, wraps itself around you with body-shape stitching. Seductively soft as a cloud, anti-allergenic, retains its elasticity.

LÖBLEIN. Drill chuck with 5 cm bore, home-handyman rapid nail driver.

BRIGITTE. Uniquely snug fit, warm and cosy, long-lasting, warm and cosy.

LÖBLEIN. High performance keyway cutter with 10 cm shank.

BRIGITTE. Non-slip dirt resistant underlay.

LÖBLEIN. Detachable jaw nut clippers.

BRIGITTE. Easy-care.

LÖBLEIN. Suction nozzle.

BRIGITTE. Kind to the skin.

LÖBLEIN. Rapid clamping.

BRIGITTE. Mothproof.

LÖBLEIN. Oh Brigitte!

BRIGITTE. Oh Karl-Otto!

LÖBLEIN. You don't understand me.

BRIGITTE. You don't understand me.

Both stand up. While Löblein pays and Brigitte puts on her coat, each sings one verse of the following song.

LÖBLEIN. To Baden did I wander,
        My passion to assuage.

Would I had not gone there,
My hopes were all dismayed.
This fire within me glowing
Is beyond all knowing.

BRIGITTE. Oft and oft I leave my skin
In water cold and hot,
Yet still there burns the fire within
What I can do I know not.
This fire within me glowing
Is beyond all knowing.

Both exit.

The stage turns into Brigitte's living-room. Brigitte on the telephone.

BRIGITTE. Brigitte Kühl speaking, Kühl as in hot. I would like to put in an advert. Heading—(*she sings*) Dream woman, smart appearance, appreciation of beautiful things, is looking for a cultured gentleman after a great disappointment. (*Speaks*) Just a moment. (*Sings*) Perhaps you too are longing for a cosy home and a cuddly woman for tender evenings. (*Speaks*) What d'you mean by that—Is the dream woman fat? Oh, I see. No, I said cuddly, not chubby. (*Sings*) Nature-loving, in need of affection. Are you too looking for a happy family, a harmonious life together? (*Speaks*) Oh no. Listen, it's better we give up this nonsense. What? Well sod off then. (*Hangs up.*) Stupid cow! (*Bursts into tears. Lights out.*)

✻ ✻ ✻

II. The Purge

CHARACTERS
Sloppo. Dictator (baritone)
Karacho. General (bass)
Mira. Sloppo's wife (soprano)

On the stage a huge bathtub on rollers, a towel rack, cans of water. Sloppo, a rather unattractive guy, is lying in the tub. Karacho, the size and shape of a gorilla, in his pyjamas with a general's uniform jacket over it. Both are singing a duet, during which Sloppo gargles and spits out water onto the floor.

DUET. Our defeats are just victories on credit.
    We will battle on—like heroes!
    And the country will fight on too—like heroes!
    And if anyone should object,
    they'll end up where the rubbish goes.
    We are the national product.
    Three cheers for our war economy!
    And should anyone disagree,
    woe to him, he's fucked.

Sloppo starts to choke while he's singing, Karacho thumps him on the back.

SLOPPO. Report, Karacho. How did it go?
    What's up? I need to know.
    Were all the traitors duly killed?

(Karacho salutes.)

    Dammit, the water's getting chilled.

Karacho adds some steaming hot water from a large jug.

    Ouch! That's murder, it's far too hot!
    Are you trying to kill me or what?
    Mira! Where are you? Mira, quick,
    I'm already pretty softened up.

Mira enters.

MIRA. Get out, Karacho, that's enough.

Exit Karacho.

SLOPPO. Why are they all against me?

MIRA. That's no surprise, Sloppo,
    it's because you're a hero, you see.

SLOPPO. Why am I always having to fight,
    having to save my skin?
    This festering sore.

MIRA. Shh! Hold your din!

SLOPPO. Because I'm always right.
    I can't help that any more.

MIRA. That's no surprise, Sloppo,
    You're a shining knight.

SLOPPO. Tell me, Mira, why then are we
    stuck out here in the back of beyond?

MIRA. A hero. The war economy.

SLOPPO. No one asks me whether I like it,
    always knowing what's what. Always me!
    Why are they all against me?

After all, I can't force them all.
After all, I can't kill them all
Just because I'm always right.

MIRA. But you can, *mon amour*,

you do it for the State.
Buck up now.
What more do you want?
For them you're Sloppo the Great.

SLOPPO. You're wrong there
I'm the one they all hate.
Just because I kill them,
they're all against me.
Just because I'm right,
They leave me in the lurch.
It really gets under my skin.
That ungrateful lot!
They're not worth a pin.

MIRA. I don't see why that should bother us,

as long as you're revered
like a shining knight.

SLOPPO. In the back of beyond.
MIRA. But still in funds.

We are the national product.

SLOPPO. Give me a scratch. Where it itches.
There! Farther down. No, on the left.

MIRA. Where's the problem?

SLOPPO. My eczema, oh how it itches!
    There! Yes! More! Keep going! Harder! Oh my angel! Oh!
MIRA. I can feel it. You're not getting any younger.
SLOPPO. I don't care any longer.
    To tell the truth, I'm fed up with it,
    I feel depressed
    I've had enough, I don't give a shit.
MIRA. What! You must be going mad.
SLOPPO. I'm giving up, I need a rest.
MIRA. Defeatist—you don't give a hoot,
    You're nothing but an empty suit!
    I'll show you, you impotent wreck,
    you're garbage, a disgrace!
    Would you like a slap on the face?
    Just now I feel the urge.
    What we really need is a purge.

She pushes him down under the water. He splutters, unable to breathe.

MIRA. They all do what you say. Except me.
    They're all afraid of you. Except me,
    you cowardly bastard!
    There's no running away, you clown,
    I'd rather let you drown—
    like a hero! Just a few minutes
    And that'll be it.

(She lets him back out of the water. Tenderly.)

No need to panic,
my little limp-dick.
You know you owe everything to me.
Yes, if I wasn't here . . .
But I'm still at your side, my dear,
you'll not get rid of me like that,
come on, my bunny, I'll sit on your lap.

(She straddles him. Gets wet.)

    Karacho, where the hell are you? Report for duty. Get a
      move on!
    And off we go.

*(Karacho enters, salutes. Mira gestures to him and he drags the
bathtub off the stage with the two of them in it. As they leave, Mira
makes the V-for-Victory sign and shouts.)*

    Disgrace! Purge! Purity!
    Glasnost!

✳ ✳ ✳

III. To Be Prepared Is the Main Thing

CHARACTERS

A prophet—dressed in black; crew cut; metal-rimmed glasses.
A small chorus of his followers gathered around him.

On a hill. Sunny day.

THE PROPHET. Truly, truly I say unto you, the sword of the Lord
    will come over the world and his vengeance will kill all who
    do not repent.

CHORUS. Truly, truly,
  the end is nigh.

THE PROPHET. Read the words written in fire on the wall and prepare your souls for the Judgement Day.

CHORUS. Truly, truly
  soon it will come.

THE PROPHET. Today, at twelve o'clock midday precisely. (*Takes
  out his pocket watch.*) In four-and-a-half minutes. Have all
  your TV licences been cancelled?

CHORUS. Cancelled.

THE PROPHET. Have you cleared out your fridges, so nothing will
  go off?

CHORUS. Cleared out.

THE PROPHET. Have you prepared your souls?

CHORUS. Prepared.

*The Prophet gives the note and brings the Chorus in. With their
weak little voices the Chorus sings: Nearer my God to Thee. The
Prophet stops them with a wave of the hand and consults his pocket
watch.*

THE PROPHET. Ten, nine, eight, seven, six, five, four, three, two,
  one . . . (*He hesitates and looks up at the sky. Drawing the words
  out.*) Four, three, two, one . . . zero!

*Pause. The members of the Chorus look at each other, check their
watches, shake their heads. One after the other they descend from
the hill. A confusion of some voices singing.*

CHORUS. Get the washing in. Don't forget—boiled ham for dinner. My credit card's expired. I just hope Putzi didn't notice anything. But what am I going to say at the office? And the dishwasher's broken down again. Now that's the holiday screwed up.

The sky darkens. It starts to rain.

THE PROPHET. (*all by himself, droning on in a grandiloquent preacher-style*). Woe unto ye of little faith.
  Woe unto ye who refuse to read the sings in the heavens.
  Woe unto ye, who cannot wait until it comes,
  the terrible end. And then, when it is too late,
  a great wailing and gnashing of teeth will arise.
  You will get what you deserve,
  when the hour of chastisement approaches.
  It's your own fault. If you had listened to me,
  while there was still time, the end of the world
  would have tasted like manna to you,
  a quiet triumph, sweet consolation
  for the Elect, with a bleak outlook
  hair loss and wet feet.

Thunder and lightning descend on the Prophet while in the distance the choir can be heard singing a ragged, out-of-tune version of the hymn 'Nearer My God to Thee'.

* * *

IV. The Opera Lover

CHARACTERS

A Singing Teacher (tenor).
A Soprano.
A married couple from the neighbourhood.

With the curtain still closed a duet can be heard—either 'Diceste questa sera la vostre preci' from Verdi's or 'Notte per me funesta' from Rossini's Otello.

The curtain rises. The setting is a typical, rather shabby, sitting-room. Glasses, cups, sheet music, a piano. In the background, an unmade bed.

The Teacher and the Soprano have reached the middle of the duet. The orchestral accompaniment is on tape. The Teacher is not sitting at the piano. He is indicating the scene with exaggerated gestures. Both are wearing improvised costumes over their everyday clothes.

Suddenly his mobile rings.

TEACHER. What's that for God's sake . . . Oh, it's you . . . Sorry, at the moment I can't . . . What? What makes you say that? Of course I'm alone . . . You must be mad . . . No! . . . I beg you . . . Yes . . . I have to ring off now . . . See you tomorrow . . . That's a promise . . . Ditto to you. (*He kisses the telephone and switches it off. Sighs.*) They can never leave you in peace.

SOPRANO. Who was that?

TEACHER. A crazy woman.

SOPRANO. You're lying. I know who it was. It was that Lizzy again. I know you.

TEACHER. Nonsense. Now we've got to get on. It's your audition the day after tomorrow. Right then . . .

(They start singing the duet again. The Teacher, now with the dagger in his hand, breaks off.) Stop, stop. C-sharp! C-sharp! Intonation weak. Nothing but squeaks. And more volume too, please. Otherwise you can forget the role.

SOPRANO. You're getting on at me all the time. You want to get rid of me. I'm certainly as good as her.

TEACHER. Now don't start getting hysterical. We'll soon sort this out.

SOPRANO. I could kill you.

TEACHER. Then go ahead and do it.

SOPRANO. You bastard.

She grabs the dagger from him. While the taped music runs on to the finale, there's a chase in which the music-stand and chairs get knocked over. Doorbell, loud knocking. They both freeze. The Teacher switches off the music and makes a run for the door. Two neighbours enter.

THE NEIGHBOURS *(in chorus)*. What's going on here? That's excessive noise. The apartment regulations! It's a crime. We're not safe in our own homes any more. We won't put up with this any longer. I'm going to ring the police radio patrol.

A threatening pose. The Teacher and the Soprano, suddenly united, go over to the attack and force the neighbours back. The Soprano threatens them with the dagger. The Teacher slams the door behind them. He laughs, belts out a love aria and throws the Soprano onto the bed.

✳ ✳ ✳

V. It's Never Too Late to Lie. A Monologue.

THE SOLOIST

A lady from the New York West Side.

Curtains closed. A voice behind the stage. Scarcely understandable jabbering, that gradually becomes clearer. We gradually start to understand it.

I confess.
I'm sorry.
Now you know but don't worry.
Affair would be saying too much.
It was just a little bit of play
and it was awful anyway.
And what is really really true,
the perfect couple is me and you.
Yes, I've hurt you, I admit—
Forget it.
But I swear to you,
The thing with that guy was just a whim
Now I'm over and done with him.

The curtain opens. The mobile rings. The woman walks up and down with her phone held to her ear.

How stupid of me,
to cause you such pain,
to be so inane
as to risk everything
for this stupid affair—
with you and me the perfect pair!
As if that was nothing.
But now I see
you're the man for me.
Why don't you come over for a drink
and then we'll dance. What d'you think?
A tango like when first we were wed,
then straight off to bed.
I get the shivers just thinking of you,
Come and hold me, oh please do.

She kisses the phone and switches it off. Loud and jubilant:

It's never too late to lie. (*Pauses*)
Now that went well enough,
he didn't even go into a huff.
Cupid gave me the idea—
Lie like a god, loud and clear.
How a man can be so naive,
so trusting, you would hardly believe.
He's already opening the champagne.
Me, I'm playing with my wedding ring.
I've always found it a pain,
The way any little thing

Can set my husband moaning again.
OK, you don't have to tell me
I'm not as young as I used to be,
but any woman who knows what's what
makes sure she never loses the plot;
innocence may be a thing of the past,
but strategy is made to last.
Hm, the problem now, *ma chère*,
is what on earth are you going to wear.

She thinks. Then she drops her wedding ring down on a plate.

Dingalingaling
So loose is my wedding ring!
Off with it.

She unbuttons her blouse and dials a number on her mobile. There's a computer on her desk. As she walks past she glances at the screen.

Yes, oh yes!
That's an end to this mess,
and an end to the lies.
I'm here for you now.
There wasn't a row,
but poor old Kenny had tears in his eyes
when I told him our marriage
wasn't working any more,
things just weren't the way they'd been before.
So it's all over now,
I'm free—and how!

Only not this evening, I've been
invited out by Pat and Doreen.
I can't get out of it.
Just a minute, I've had an idea.
Why not now, at my place, here?
Come and let's have some fun,
I'm waiting, my blouse already undone.

A notification sound from the computer announcing a new email.

An urgent email.
This blasted machine
Always keeps you on the go
I'll ring back in a mo.

Kisses the phone and switches off.

It's never too late to lie.

She reads the message on the screen.

Oh, it's that René
asking if we should meet
for lunch in a cafe?
Why not? Now what did he say?
'Loves walking, opera fan, gourmet.'
That sounds like a man
In the prime of life
The photo's not bad, nice tan,
Obviously bored with his wife.

She types, letter by letter, on her keyboard

Just tell me when and where.

A little lunch, that's what you said.
OK. Age is neither here nor there.
From what I hear the young guys
aren't so good in bed.
Round the corner there's a cafe.
Look forward to seeing you, René.

Switches off the computer.

Whoopee!

Picks up the phone again, thinks for a moment, then keys in a number.

Darling, oh, it's such a pain,
I have to nip to the office again.
I'd forgotten that when we spoke,
I don't even get time for a sandwich and coke!
But it'll only be until three,
Then there'll be time for you and me.
I'll come right round, you'll see—
Be sure to send your butler out—
I'll have you nude in no time at all
and then we'll have a ball
on your stylish Bauhaus couch.
And if you tie me up, I'll shout ouch!
Let's leave it at that—see you soon.

She rings off and goes to the mirror to check how she looks.

A femme fatale
bewitching all,
fancy free,

yes, that's me,
never stuck
with just one buck
there's plenty of room in my heart.

She touches up her lipstick.

Who do these guys think they are?
They're charmed
But they're not that smart.

The slurping as she rubs the lipstick over her mouth is audible.

I've got to be on my way. Ah!

Suddenly there's a loud ring at the door.

Who's there?
Is it you, Kenny?
Ted?
My latest, now what was he called?

Shots can be heard. She screams.

My God! Can it be all three?
Shooting each other because of me?
Out of jealousy?
Damn it!
It's flattering, that's true at least,
But it doesn't leave me in peace.

She sits down at her computer again, fiddles with the mobile phone. As she does so she sings, very softly this time.

Now I'm quite distraught
How quickly you can become a widow! Alack!

Yes, I know what one ought
To wear—from now on it'll be black

She puts her wedding ring back on.

What a strong guy my Kenny was. A bull of a man.
My poor heart, it's broken.
And René too, a real gentleman.
I do wish we could have spoken.
And now you've left me all alone
But I'll think of you, the men I've known,
Here in my solitary state.

There's hammering in the door.

The police! I can hardly wait!

A few hours later. Her hair-do shows signs of her agitation. She's still wearing the same dress.

Those shots, I really should have known—
Just kids out there, and they were stoned.
Who'd shoot himself for my sake anyway?
All this has really messed up my day.
Now I've missed out on lunch, I fear.
I put Kenny off with a flea in his ear
And the other one's forgotten our date.
Then, dammit! now I'm far too late
for my rendezvous again—
getting old really is a pain.

She wails.

I've got this buzzing noise in my ears,

things just keep getting worse with the years.

There's a quiet ring at the door. She's surprised, goes over hesi-
tantly, almost reluctantly, and has a look through the peephole.
She whispers.

It's you. You!

She slowly recovers her composure.

What's all this?
Coming home early from work.
And there was me, almost frantic.
My husband's such a romantic!

She opens the door. Her relief is visibly genuine.

Goodness me! Now give me a kiss.

Curtain.

La boîte

It is presumably well known that the Germans can't stand their own stars. In the past they were simply driven out, today they're acclaimed abroad. And only when they're on the red carpet in Hollywood or Cannes do we try to bring them back. That is not only true of the cinema but also of the stage. Ingrid Cavan has retreated entirely to Paris, where she performs to full houses. That's not important, of course, things can be very nice away from home. I admire her and have written a few songs for her now and then. When she had a new idea, I didn't need to be asked twice. She wondered whether I fancied contriving a pocket opera for her.

I wanted to know what she meant by that. 'You know how expensive and involved everything is in places like Bayreuth and Salzburg,' she said. 'Small is beautiful. What I have in mind is something transportable that doesn't cost too much. An opera or, as we used to say in German, a *Singspiel*, with three or four characters, a set you can fold away and a tiny orchestra, let's say four or five instruments, that's enough. You could even take something like that on tour.'

I just laughed at her. 'Don't you know that it's easier to raise a million than the derisory sum you need for something like that. The managers, who call the tune in your industry, prefer expensive projects.'

But there's nothing you wouldn't do for a good friend, who's a star into the bargain.

Ingrid soon found the most important person for her project, the composer. He's called Oscar Strasnoy and was born in Buenos Aires, 40 years ago. He'd made a name for himself as a pianist and conductor as well. Luciano Berio awarded him the Orpheus Prize in Spoleto for his opera *Midea*. His cantata *Hochzeitsvorbereitungen* (Wedding Preparations), based on Kafka's story, had its first performance in 2000, later came his *Opérette* on a libretto by Witold Gombrowicz, the operas: *Le Bal*, based on a story by Irène Némirovsky in Hamburg; and *Un Retour*, with a libretto by Alberto Manguel in Aix-en-Provence. Oscar lives in Paris and Berlin.

What came out of all this is our pocket opera *La boîte*. Structurally the piece has the form of a revue presenting the biography of a female singer. Ingrid Cavan plays the leading role. In each scene two men appear, a pair of theatrical twins who each take several roles. The pair of them are like Dr Jekyll and Mr Hyde or the good cop and the bad cop. These two demons serve the singer, seduce her, promote her, exploit her: officer, manager, lover, patron, costumier, musician. Discreet echoes of real people are possible. Apart from them, there is a third man who sits at the side of the stage working on a typewriter and occasionally reading out some of what he has written. His role is that of an announcer or an MC.

At the very beginning, the twins drag a box onto the stage. This *boîte* is at once a suitcase, a treasure chest, a wardrobe, a coffin, a hiding place—similar to the chest in which a woman is sawn in half. All the props and costumes are taken out of this box. The production, stage set and costumes should make the distance in time from the present visible. The action is set roughly between 1943 and 1990.

The first scenes show a little girl growing up in an industrial district (the Saarland). She makes her debut as a singer one Christmas Eve when she appears before Wehrmacht soldiers. After the war she ekes out a living on the black market. Two officers of the army of occupation, a Frenchman and an American, court her. The Frenchman manages to secure a first engagement for her in Paris. But a successful career is merely incidental to the play. It's more about pain, strange games, turf wars and self-doubt. You could call it a tragi-comedy of art. Here are a few scenes that might give an idea of what it's about:

Fifth Number. Pain, Saarland, 1950

Hospital ward. The twins as Doctor and Male Nurse. The Singer in a clinical chair. She has a rosary in her hand. She's scratching herself. The Doctor is dictating his diagnosis to his secretary.

Three musical elements: a doctor's song, a nursery rhyme repeated mechanically and three stanzas from the Stabat Mater— *the composer can choose which version to use: Palestrina, Orlando di Lasso, Pergolesi, Haydn, Schubert . . .*

DOCTOR. The patient's reading from the Bible
    which suggests she's highly liable
    to ecclesiogenous conditions
    affecting her without remission:
    squama, urtica, oedema
    dermatological eczema.

SINGER. *Stabat mater dolorosa*
    juxta crucem lacrimosa
    dum pendebat filius,
    cuius animam gementem
    contristatam et dolentem
    pertransivit gladius.

DOCTOR (*turning to the patient*). Don't worry, my little jenny wren,
    we'll soon have you on your feet again,
    and back where you belong.
    But what's the point of all these songs?

In the meantime, the nurse has started to wrap the patient in white bandages, starting with her feet. By the end of the scene she's completely encased in them. She tries to free her ears. She can no longer finish the Stabat Mater because the bandages cover her mouth. With a shrill note she gets up out of the chair.

NURSE (*chanting like a nursery rhyme*). What's the use, you silly goose? Look—first comes the Vaseline, then bandages to keep it clean. That'll cure you of your itch, but just stay still, you little witch. None of your monkey business here, or you'll be thrown out on your ear.

SINGER. *Sancta mater, istud agas,*
   crucifixi fige plagas
   cordi meo valide.
   Tui nati vulnerati
   iam dignati pro me pati,
   poenas mecum divide!

DOCTOR. This music's just an irritation,
   I prescribe its termination.
   The allergies affecting your skin
   Require the strictest discipline.

NURSE. Come on, Chick, you're making me sick. All your tralalas are a pain in the arse. You're really a pest, give this scratching a rest. Look—first comes the Vaseline, then bandages to keep it clean. That'll cure you of your itch, but just stay still, you little witch. None of your monkey business here, or you'll be thrown out on your ear.

SINGER. *Virgo virginum praeclara*
   mihi iam non sis amara,
   fac me tecum plangere,
   fac ut portem . . .

The bandages have reached her mouth and silence her while she's singing.

Ninth Number. The Transformation, Paris, 1965

On an almost completely darkened stage only the outlines of the chest can be made out. Sung measurements such as 38, 42, 82, then, say, waist 82 or hips 96 can be heard. They are the voices of the Twins who in this scene appear as a Couturier and his assistant. The light strikes the bare back of a statue—but no it is, as will appear, the Singer. The two of them are dancing around her. Mirrors on all sides. The Assistant takes rolls of cloth, scissors, a measuring tape, needles out of the chest. A brief dialogue between Couturier and Assistant—measurements and commands are repeatedly sung: 'Do be careful,'—'Idiot!'—'No, higher. Are you blind?' The couturier is impatient, his assistant obedient but secretly rebellious. At the end, a piece of cloth being torn can be heard.

Change of lighting. Couturier alone. He seems to be working on the Singer who is standing, as before, with her back to the audience. Music.

COUTURIER. You just can't keep still.—The drape's not right.—
This cloth is no use at all.—Damn and blast it!

He works himself up into a fury and belabours the bare back beside him. It's a tailor's dummy. It falls over. The head comes off and rolls across the floor. Blackout.

Fade-in. Music: Introduction to the following song. The Singer in a luxurious evening gown. The Assistant adjusts the train. The Couturier is happy with it. Walking around among the clothes, shoes and underwear on the floor, she sings the Song of the Avatar to the

mirror. The Assistant dashes to and fro behind her, adjusting this
or that detail.

SINGER. Do you too have the feeling
    that nothing suits you,
    that it's tight, catches and scratches,
    that the *drape's* not right?
    My suitcase, this container here,
    is full of things:
    chinchilla fur, petticoat, apron,
    uniform, wedding dress, bikini—
    All of it wrong, all a mistake.
    What you see here
    is just a mannequin,
    waiting for something that fits,
    something to bring it to life.
    As a monster, for all I care—
    queen, hussy, gambler, avatar.
    Every one of those,
    and its opposite.
    I'd like to be myself. At last!
    This other woman by the mirror
    is me.

As the song finishes the Singer ends up in front of the mirror.
Blackout.

Twelfth Number. The Song of the Box

The stage is empty apart from a piano. The applause dies away. We hear the journalist typing. From the wings we hear a vehement argument between the Singer and the Twins in the roles of the Lover and the Impresario. Acoustic chaos—ad lib. Cries, a bottle breaking, curses, obscenities. It's all about money, fraud, corruption, jealously and her career.

SINGER (*shouts*). Quiet! I can't hear myself speak, I can't hear
    anything at all.

She goes on stage wearing headphones. Throws all the paraphernalia back in the chest, sits down and listens to some music until the audience starts getting restless. Then she stands up and takes off the headphones.

SINGER. Look, ladies and gentlemen,
    at this box here.
    At some time or other a box like this
    is waiting for every one of you,
    a safe, a case, a chest.
    As I'm sure you can see.

    But there's never any rest,
    ladies and gentlemen,
    at least not for me.
    As a woman I need
    my pills, my splendid shoes,
    my nail varnish, the things I use.

I lug them around with me
in this crate, my *boîte*,
my basket, my chest,
my box. It's my nightspot,
my *étui*, my *nécessaire*,
until I've a bit more time to spare.

Ladies and gentlemen,
sometimes I can't go on any more,
sometimes I'm fed up with everything.
Do you feel like that? You don't?
You're quite content, in your abode there?
You never feel you want to get out?
Out of your *étui*? Out on a spree?
Out of the house and in the fresh air?
On, come on now.
It was great to see you all,
here in this little hall.

She goes over to the piano and closes the lid. Blackout. The end.

The lid was then very audibly slammed down on our pocket opera in Berlin and it happened like this: Peter Mussbach, artistic director of the Berlin State Opera at the time, was interested in taking it on; he was even going to direct it himself. In March 2008, he invited us to a see him in his spacious office in order to discuss the details of the production which was planned for November of that year. The libretto was ready, the leading singer had arrived from Paris, the composer, Oscar Strasnoy, was well known. He had been asked to compose the score in time. The artistic director has a big say in what happens in an opera house, but he needs the support of his people and so Mussbach had invited his general administrator, his head of opera and his dramaturg to be there. Dates and fees were agreed, no one opposed the agreements. But there was one thing we hadn't reckoned with and that was the so-called Opera Foundation in Berlin in which all sorts of the great and the good call the tune. We had no idea that one of the usual backstage theatre intrigues was going on. In fact only a few months later Peter Mussbach was hounded out of his post. Naive as we were, we still thought the State Opera would honour the agreements, but that was out of the question. The new interim director bluntly informed us that the project had been scrapped and there was no question of the promised fees being paid.

Then the lawyers got to work. Peter Mussbach wrote to us: 'The day before yesterday I spoke to Ingrid Caven on the phone and she told me she intended to sue the State Opera. I have to tell you that I can not only understand that but also find it "right and proper"—after all, we made a binding contractual agreement for the *La Boîte* project in the presence of the most important members of the so-called company. Should you wish to get in touch with me in connection with this blasted case, I will naturally support you—it is about the facts and not some petty act of revenge—even with a sell-out, you have to behave decently.'

There followed convoluted writs and submissions of evidence. The Berlin District Court was called in; they came to the Solomonic judgement that all that was due was our share of the costs. Two weeks later, the State Opera Foundation refused to accept any judicial settlement, probably with the aim of greatly increasing the lawyers' fees and other legal expenses for the artists involved. The administrators are covered against such risks, since when they lose cases it is not they who are liable for the costs but the taxpayer. Anyone who realizes that is well advised to avoid any contact with such people.

So much for that particular failure. Further weighty negotiations with other theatres followed. An intelligent and vivacious woman, responsible for the programme of the Ruhr Festival, insisted on making a firm booking for the pocket opera for the forthcoming season. Anyone who knew her was baffled when one day she killed herself, without warning and without leaving a farewell letter. The new administration of the Festival failed to remember any of the commitments she'd made.

At present, when I am reviewing these long-forgotten catastrophes, lies and machinations, there is talk of a production in French, in which it is said that the Théâtre National du Luxembourg and the Parisian Bouffes du Nord will combine. Once more Peter Mussbach is keen to direct it. *À la bonne heure.*

My Failed Theatrical Projects

The Tortoise

My first flop as a playwright didn't come on stage. It happened in a nineteenth-century hunting lodge. Göhrde, a building that had more of a shack than a castle, is in the Lüchow-Dannenberg district, not far from the old border with East Germany, an out-of-the-way place that later became famous for the protests against the planned permanent repository for nuclear waste in Gorleben.

In 1961, Hans Werner Richter invited the notorious informal writers' association Gruppe 47 to one of its conferences. He had a liking for such grotesque places where the walls were covered in antlers and the mine host more conversant with beer and schnapps than wine. One of the rituals of these meetings was that we sat in the 'electric chair' to read out from unpublished works.

I had brought my play, 'The Tortoise'. The title referred to an aged federal chancellor who clung on to office with astonishing determination. Two schoolboys who were annoyed at conditions prevailing at the time, managed to kidnap the distinguished statesman. In the Fifties, the idea of terrorism sounded exotic. Inoffensiveness was the order of the day. The worst the security forces expected was the odd tomato, which mostly missed its target. The criminal energy of the desperados who, a decade later, gave themselves the grandiose title of Red Army, was still in the distant future.

After their successful capture of the poor Chancellor, the two schoolboys were faced with the question of what to do with him. In conversation their victim turned out to be a man who, with a mixture of understanding and guile, kept driving them into a corner, until eventually all they wanted to do was to get rid of the old gentleman. My ambition was to present the operation of the two amateurs as a comedy—unfortunately I've forgotten how I went about it. The manuscript no longer exists, which I regard as all to the good.

My reading in Göhrde lasted a good quarter of an hour. I can't recall a single titter from the audience. They listened in silence which I attributed to their keen attentiveness until H. W. Richter interrupted me, in the tones of a benign grandfather, with the words, 'I think that's enough. We'll have a break now.' How civilized things were in those days can be seen from the fact that none of the critics rose to speak. With that 'The Tortoise' was silently but permanently laid to rest.

Parvus

My next theatre project that got nowhere was about Lenin. But the lack of response wasn't aimed at me personally. The simple fact was that no one was interested in a subject like that. Always these old left-wing stories. Gorki's *Mother*, the eternal *Battleship Potemkin*, Peter Weiss with his *Trotsky*, a 'contribution to the Lenin Year 1970'—it was all old hat.

I begged to differ. I didn't like the post-revolutionary hangover of the 1970s, it was understandable but not material for a full-length playscript. Wasn't there still something there that hadn't been dealt with? I came across two books that made me wonder: Wilfried B. Scharlau and Zbnyek A. Zeman: *The Merchant of the Revolution: The Life of Alexander Israel Helphand (Parvus) 1867–1924* (London, 1965), and Alexander Solzhenitsyn: *Lenin in Zurich* (New York, 1976). So it all started in the middle of the First World War, I thought. A powerful subject for the stage, I thought, even if no one was interested in it. Something to keep in reserve, then. Pity really. At least here I can show how I saw the exposition:

CHARACTERS

Alexander Israel Helphand, also known as Parvus
Yekaterina, his constant companion
Georg Skarz, his adjutant and factotum
Jakob Fürstenberg, also known as Hanecki, Bolshevist agent in Parvus' service
Alice Brøgger, a friend of Parvus', a courtesan
Vladimir Ilyich Ulyanov, better known as Lenin
Madame de K., his lover
Ulrich, Count von Brockdorff-Rantzau, German envoy to Copenhagen
Babette, a cook
Rodolphe, Lenin's assistant and bodyguard

The ground floor of a country house in the Canton of Zurich. Morning. Babette is polishing the floor. Rodolphe is hanging up curtains.

RODOLPHE. What will the master and mistress say about that?

BABETTE. Oh, them. (*Imitating them.*) A total lack of taste. (*Laughs.*)

RODOLPHE. What's so funny? These tenants are turning the house upside down.

BABETTE. They can go ahead for all I care.

RODOLPHE. The man's crazy, that much is obvious.

BABETTE. But he's got piles of money. Our master and mistress on the other hand . . .

RODOLPHE. You don't understand. Now shut up and come and hold the rod for me.

BABETTE. Do you know what he said to me? He'll take me with them. To Denmark. He's got a house by the sea.

RODOLPHE. You'd be stupid to fall for that. He's a con man. I saw that right away. The way he's refurbishing the house. They're expecting someone.

BABETTE. Who would that be?

RODOLPHE. I'll find out soon enough. He's going on as if it was a state visit. He's a carpetbagger. Just you wait, I'll soon see what he's up to. (*Exeunt.*)

Parvus enters.

PARVUS. The smell in here! Musty. Gone down in the world. Skarz! Where on earth are you? (*Skarz enters.*) Switzerland really drives you crazy. That lake out there. It's just too quiet here. It's high time we got away. The day after tomorrow, early in the morning, if everything goes as it should. The Balkan deals in Zurich the day after tomorrow, two new accounts. Are you even listening to me, Skarz? What does it look like upstairs? The guest room?

SKARZ. Like in a sarcophagus.

PARVUS. Good. Get the pictures dusted. As much oil as possible. (*Exit Skarz.*) And don't forget to tell the cook.

YEKATERINA. Your Skarz is messing everything up. A creature of habit. He should stick to his desk. Leave all that to me. You need to rest.

PARVUS. You can save your concern—you'll end up killing me with it.

YEKATERINA. Alexander!

PARVUS. OK, OK. Let's forget it. You know what the point of all this is. What's important is that he comes. Once I've got him here, nothing can go wrong. I've got everything ready. He has to have the feeling he's entering enemy territory. That's good. The whole house is a nightmare. He mustn't feel comfortable here.

YEKATERINA. And what do you want to achieve with that?

PARVUS. I can still remember going for a walk with him in London. *Their* houses, *their* fairness, *their* restaurants—he always spat that out. He spat on everything I liked. So I'll play the parvenu. It's not difficult for me, after all I am a parvenu. And then, when he's rigid with hatred, on his guard, every muscle tensed up, I'll offer him precisely the thing he needs. He can't say no. He needs me. He needs me for one afternoon. Then we'll see how things go.

YEKATERINA. If he actually does come.

PARVUS. And the German. A calculation with two unknowns. Leave me by myself. Where's Hanecki? (*Exit Yekaterina.*) Hanecki!

HANECKI. You called?

PARVUS. How are things going?

HANECKI. It's all arranged. The German's coming at three.

PARVUS. You spoke to him yourself?

HANECKI. Do you imagine Jakob Fürstenberg would allow himself to be fobbed off with a clerk?

PARVUS. The envoy was in his usual state?

HANECKI. Woebegone.

PARVUS. There you are, then. (*Enter Alice.*) You look magnificent. (*Exit Hanecki.*)

ALICE. I do, do I? I feel wretched. You smell of cod liver oil. This whole enterprise smells of cod liver oil. Even the house. Rancid.

PARVUS. Slept badly?

ALICE. I'm not going along with this.

PARVUS. You should have thought of that sooner. I need you. That dress won't do.

ALICE. Parvus the *stage director*.

PARVUS. It's too ordinary.

ALICE. You regard me as a sweet. Wrapped in glossy paper.

PARVUS. Alice, dear, we're here to work.

ALICE. What you understand by work. You should leave me in peace.

PARVUS. He'll be suspicious.

ALICE. Justifiably suspicious.

PARVUS. I've set up this whole business entirely to his advantage.

ALICE. How altruistic.

PARVUS. I'm not going to earn a single kopek from it.

ALICE. At least not directly.

PARVUS. So he'll look for the catch.

ALICE. And that won't take him long.

PARVUS. How come?

ALICE. How come? If he gets involved with the Germans, you'll have him over a barrel. Do you imagine he has any desire to let himself be blackmailed by you? By you of all people? I'll warn him.

PARVUS. There's no need for that.

ALICE. Perhaps he'll be grateful to me.

PARVUS. Are you serious about this? You're declaring war on me? Staying here? Working for Ulyanov?

ALICE. That wouldn't be a bad idea.

PARVUS. Do you think I hadn't noticed what's going on inside your tiny head? But you're in for a big surprise, Alice. You won't get much out of your new friends. They won't be setting up houses on the Öresund for you. You can pack your things and go.

ALICE. I'm staying here.

PARVUS. Listen, Alice. I know you. How long ago is it that I picked you up on the Nyhavn? With your funny hat and your black veil I could see at once that you were an intelligent girl. I'm never wrong about these things.

ALICE. Useful—in every respect.

PARVUS. Unhappy with things and eager, like myself. Empty-handed but with a head full of ideas. Interested in things. Quick on the uptake.

ALICE. Oh, do stop.

PARVUS. I trained you.

ALICE. You could call it that.

PARVUS. And you were good. Very good.

ALICE. And now I've had enough.

PARVUS. Because you can't stay still. You imagine there's more in life for you. Something I can't offer. And now you have the feeling you can get it from Ulyanov and his people. Go ahead, for all I care. Try it. I know them. I went along with them for ten years and I can tell you they'll exploit you in quite a different way from me. They'll suck you dry and they expect you to carry on with shining eyes. And the tighter their hold on you, the more devotion they'll expect.

ALICE. But no devotion to some cheap deal.

PARVUS. No, they deal in blood and bones.

ALICE. Only not for their own pockets.

PARVUS. And all the worse for that. I can already see you in the one-room flat. And definitely in clink. Those guys are always going to jail. OK, then, you try it. Go to bed with the revolution—and have an enjoyable evening.

ALICE. That's what I was supposed to be doing anyway.

PARVUS. Oh yes, of course. You know what—have a good look at him and do whatever you want. But off you go now. And put a different dress on.

ALICE. You really do smell of cod liver oil. Funny, I've never noticed that before.

They embrace. Exit Alice.

Later. Doorbell rings, Parvus answers it. Two bodyguards, behind them Ulyanov.

PARVUS. Good morning, Vladimir Ilyich. Have you breakfasted? Do sit down.

ULYANOV (*nods to Parvus, then glances at the furnishings, laughs*). Whom does this house belong to?

PARVUS. That's neither here nor there.

ULYANOV. Are they reliable?

PARVUS. Even better. They're completely unsuspecting.

ULYANOV. How many people are there in the house?

PARVUS. Everything as agreed. My wife, Yekaterina. Hanecki— surely you know Hanecki? Then old Skarz. And my assistant Alice. Alice Brøgger. Delightful woman.

ULYANOV. Hmm.

PARVUS. Grumpy as ever. You can relax, Vladimir Ilyich. Even being on the alert can turn into a bad habit.

ULYANOV. Well, I still don't want any witnesses. (*Waves at the bodyguards, they exit.*)

PARVUS. No one knows about our discussion. Every one of us will deny it ever took place. You don't trust me. That's normal. But you have come. That's intelligent.

ULYANOV. And what do you have to offer?

PARVUS. You know very well what I have to offer, otherwise you wouldn't be here. I'm offering you the Germans and that means firstly, money for the Party, money for the revolution. And secondly, your transit to Scandinavia on a day you decide. The conditions have to be negotiated. The German envoy to Copenhagen is coming this afternoon. He's coming alone and has full authorization.

ULYANOV. I don't negotiate with the Germans.

PARVUS. I know that you have made contact, but your contacts there are subordinates. That's pointless. You need someone to work for you since, as you say, you 'don't negotiate with the Germans.' I'll undertake that for you.

ULYANOV. There's no point in us trying to pull the wool over each other's eyes, Parvus. I've made enquiries about you.

PARVUS. Party gossip. Emigrants' tittle-tattle.

ULYANOV. Your Balkan affairs. Your attempts to meddle in the Ukrainian and Bulgarian movement. Your shady deals in Denmark. Your kowtowing to the German general staff. And so on. You are a German agent.

PARVUS. You still underestimate me. As you always have done.

ULYANOV. Even back in 1902 I realized that you were a renegade.

PARVUS. I'm delighted that you remember our time together in Schwabing, Vladimir Ilyich. Even back then you underestimated me. I'm surprised you still think you can intimidate me with your homemade anathemas—renegade, rascally knave, lackey of capital. Let's not keep trotting out the same old tune. Do you still remember how we printed out *Iskra* back then? In my apartment. We didn't have a penny. The printer was left empty-handed. When will you finally come to understand what the old Jew in London saw—a revolution costs money. You're still the same as you were then—still the same fear of money, still fascinated by it. You find it uncanny, don't you?

ULYANOV. You're a dealer, Parvus. What are the Germans actually paying you for your services?

PARVUS. I've got enough money. I don't need money. Quite the opposite of you. Can't we put this shadow-boxing behind us and get on to business? Right then—the Germans are interested in a Russian revolution. The sooner and more radical it is, the better. Then the eastern front will collapse. [. . .]

ULYANOV Right then, we'll see about that this afternoon. You like danger, I don't.

PARVUS. Tomorrow you can get back to your old tomes in the National Library. In the meantime, we'll enjoy the partridges.

ULYANOV. What annoys me most, Parvus, is that I like you. Sometimes I regret that people like you are going to have to disappear.

PARVUS. You like me because I'm of use to you. You even forgive me for serving you partridges. Come with me.

End of Act One.

The Daughter of the Air

'For me it's the most magnificent of all Calderón's plays,' Goethe said, ascribing 'incredible judgement in construction, genius in invention' to the writer. How can it be that *The Daughter of the Air* has never become established in the theatre, at least in Germany? One fine day, when I had nothing better to do, I set to work not just to understand that, but to change it. Once finished, I described the procedure I had chosen:

The Spanish original consists of two full-length parts, both in five *jornadas*, or acts, and in its original form each part takes four or five hours. It displays all the fruits of a golden age of ceremonial and rhetoric. The plot is elaborate but also extravagant, over-ornate and wearying with its many repetitions. In the dialogue the foreign king addresses Semiramis, the legendary Queen of Babylon, in no less than 240 lines of verse and her reply is hardly any shorter. In structure, baroque court theatre is not averse to pauses in the action, digressions and repeats. Mythological allusions are dredged up, prehistories related and opera-like recitatives inserted with no regard for the situation on stage.

For that reason a new translation could not rescue the play—and that even less the more faithful it was. My first step, therefore, was a ruthless reduction. Layer by layer I cleared away the wording of the play in order to reconstruct it scene by scene.

Anyone who regards this attempt to win back Calderón for the theatre as scavenging should at least have a look at the Spanish original; they will find that it is more a tribute to the author's inventiveness. Nothing was farther from my mind than to bring a classic up to date. For me an art that tries to prove its boldness by slaughtering pigs on the stage or urinating on crucifixes is doomed to play to empty houses. Adapters and directors who spend their time trampling over some source material or other are wasting their time; there will be a striking disparity between their strong-arm tactics and the results. Just as in the art market, the marginal aesthetic benefit of sacrilege drops close to zero.

My work was, therefore, based on a stylistic principle that you could call *polemical classicism*. Its linguistic form is verse. In plays verse does not claim to rule over the text. It doesn't want to attract attention to itself, but to what is being shown. In that way it aids the linguistic *mise-en-scène*. As in the original it determines, to a certain extent, the gestures, level and tone of the dialogue. In accordance with this functional purpose, I chose a particularly flexible metre: the three- or four-foot iambus. The result is a kind of 'floating' blank verse. This discreet and rather sober verse-form is intended not to increase the fantastic nature of the plot but to subvert it.

From a distance of a few hundred years, it is not difficult to see what is etiquette, convention, custom in a sonata, building or play—in fact it's all too easy. On the other hand, to perceive the risks taken, that are enclosed in tradition, like an insect in amber, demands a certain degree of imagination. But the way Calderón's demonstration of the problematic nature of the legitimacy of the crown, his exposure of its unlimited power, the heathen substratum of his tragedy, the unbridled treatment of the problems of sexuality—all of that blows the limits of courtly theatre apart, indeed it even threatens the author's ideological and religious premisses. There are energies at work here that are beyond his conscious control, allowing him to proceed on his somnambulistic way all the more surely. The attraction, the danger of transformation, that can go as far as the dissociation of the self, seems demonic; panic-stricken the notion of finding oneself trapped that recurs like a nightmare in the image of the cave and the figure of the chained-up dog (bitch).

Not the least of Calderón's bold strokes lies in his avoidance of limiting himself to what is probable. This leads to some of his best effects. The fact that Semiramis is literally the image of her son not only creates the prerequisites for one of the most stupendous double roles in world literature, the idea also leads to a 'confusion of feelings' (to quote Stefan Zweig) that goes so far and has such inescapable consequences that it is almost unique in the theatre. Almost but not entirely. Two dramatists were bold enough to try something similar: Shakespeare and Heinrich von Kleist.

There was actually a first production of this play in 1992. It was in Essen and the director was Hansgünther Heyme; it was followed by a few productions in Bremen and elsewhere. In spite of that I am happy to include *The Daughter of the Air* in the list of my flops. Hardly anyone will deny that culture is a stochastic process—and in this case, just as well, a scarcely foreseeable random event occurred. This is how it came about.

In 1999, the Burgtheater in Vienna planned a new production. That was fine and for two reasons. In fact that theatre was where the play belonged; what other stage than the old 'Imperial and Royal' Burgtheater could help bring about a renaissance for Calderón? And secondly, they had an extremely gifted dramaturg, Wolfgang Wiens. He had all sorts of objections to my work and saw to it that, on his advice, I wrote a Viennese version of the play which dealt with these. The magnificent Andrea Breth was engaged as director. It was known that she occasionally suffered sudden dangerous attacks of melancholia. That happened again a few weeks before the opening night and she had to call off. However, the programme was set in concrete. The artistic director's telephone was never silent. Eventually a saviour was found in the person of Frank Castorf, the head of the Berliner Volksbühne, who was willing to step in at once. Unfortunately, it was impossible to fit in sufficient rehearsal time so the director went ahead and amputated the play.

Fortunately, the theatre had the sensitivity not to invite me to the premiere. That spared me some annoyance for, as I was told, there was nothing much left of Calderón's play other than the prelude. So even though Castorf was one of the favourites of theatre critics, *The Daughter of the Air* was taken off after a few performances.

Calderón de la Barca will survive it. Below are a few of his lines:

Wilderness. Outside the entrance to a cave. Semiramis, Tiresias, Chato.

SEMIRAMIS. Tiresias! Tiresias!

TIRESIAS. What are you shouting for?

SEMIRAMIS. Air!

TIRESIAS. What do you want?

SEMIRAMIS. Set me free.

TIRESIAS (*to Chato*). Open the door for her, old chap,
    but keep a close eye on her.
    You mustn't let her escape.

SEMIRAMIS. You are my second father,
    my lackey, guardian, saviour.
    Release me from this dungeon.
    I've lived for long enough
    trapped in the dark, like a dog.
    You're turning this wilderness—
    my cradle—into my tomb.

TIRESIAS. How often must I tell you, no,
    it's not of my volition,
    that you are here. The Goddess,
    as you well know, commanded me to do it,
    to save you, and to save the world
    from you, Semiramis.
    Violent was your begetting
    and violence brought about your birth.

SEMIRAMIS. Yes!

TIRESIAS. The signs of the constellations
    proclaim that you are the virgin,
    the bringer of death, the whore
    of Babylon, who sows violence,
    and, so they say, who will come
    to a violent end.

SEMIRAMIS. Yes!

TIRESIAS. Whole nations across the world
    you will crush beneath your feet
    and behead many people. Your beauty
    will dazzle the man who desires you
    and for the man who gives you his hand
    love will be as a poison.
    Is it this that you seek?

SEMIRAMIS. Yes! My desire is to rise
    and breathe the higher air.

TIRESIAS. Tell me why this is.

SEMIRAMIS. You may believe the stars
    old man. The cave that you guard
    you have dug out for yourself,
    not for me, out of fear. But I,
    Semiramis, am a match
    for any portent. Here within me
    is enough of strength and reason
    to ward it off. Cowardice it is
    to choose death simply
    in order to live. Let children
    shiver at the sound of thunder
    I wait for the lightning bolt.

Distant music.

TIRESIAS (*to Chato*). She's struggling, hold her fast.

SEMIRAMIS. Nothing can hold me. Let go,
    or my rage will turn me into
    my own executioner
    and you, Tiresias, will see
    me dead through your own fault.

TIRESIAS. Never was she so out of
    her mind. What should I do?
    How comes it that she has awoken
    from the deep sleep her life has been
    all of a sudden?

SEMIRAMIS. What?
    Can you not hear it? Have you
    gone deaf in your old age?

That is the high note of the
future awakening me.
Music it is that threatens,
lures and speaks of all
this wilderness lacks,
of what bewilders me
and what is calling me,
of power and love.

TIRESIAS. Come, Chato, and help me
bind her, then close the door.

Semiramis is locked up again.

Without Us. A Dialogue of the Dead.

In an army camp in the backwoods of Malaysia two veterans are sitting in a hut with two camp-beds and two chairs. One is in his mid-sixties, English, an investment banker; his speculations led to the collapse of a big London bank—the one I had in mind was Nick Leeson, who fled after the debacle and escaped to Borneo. The other man, Thomas, is German and in his late forties; he used to be a member of a terrorist group in Berlin and was later busted as a drug courier in Malaysia. They've been forgotten, as has the commandant of the remote camp, who is waiting in vain for instructions from the capital. It is hot. Rain is drumming on the corrugated-iron roof.

THOMAS. Actually it was only the women who were really fanatical about the cause. We men clung to our weapons because there was nothing else left. We kept up our campaign out of a permanent feeling that attack was the best form of defence. Going underground—d'you know what that means?

Claustrophobia and paranoia. In the group everyone was suspicious of everyone else. Traitors everywhere, especially among your own people. Eventually we were each sending the other to the slaughter.

Do you think I would have got involved in that drug business of my own free will? The group spent all its time talking about logistics. Safe houses. Getting money. All means allowed when it's for the cause. And when I was arrested, in Kuala Lumpur, my comrades abandoned me.

PHILIP (*laughs*). Yes. It doesn't take long for that to happen. Overnight you're yesterday's man. I could tell you a thing or two about that. Funny. On Monday I was the *Master of the Universe*, on Tuesday no one wanted to know me any more. Wife gone, money gone, passport gone.

THOMAS. Exactly. Then the headlines, first item in the evening news, old photos everywhere—it goes on for a week, then you're forgotten. The secret service beat me up till I was almost dead. They gave me a good going-over for three whole days. The Embassy, the Red Cross, Amnesty International—none of them put in an appearance.

PHILIP. I know, I know. You told me that years ago. Why can't you let it be, Thomas? I'll tell you why. Because those were our glory days. Old soldiers' tales. We haven't got any others. Nothing's going to happen to us any more.

THOMAS. We're in the same boat.

PHILIP. On dry land.

The following litany, a kind of 'speaking in tongues', slowly intensifies, becoming faster and louder until it is incomprehensible.

PHILIP. Victory in the people's war!

THOMAS. Portfolio management!

PHILIP. Freedom for the Basque country!

THOMAS. An injection of liquidity!

PHILIP. The Shining Path!

THOMAS. Offshore banking!

PHILIP. For the Islamic revolution!

THOMAS. Derivatives from derivatives!

PHILIP. Smash the things that smash you!

THOMAS. The London Interbank Offering Rate!

PHILIP. Freedom for all political prisoners!

THOMAS. Nikkei, Nasdaq, Euro Stoxx!

PHILIP. International solidarity!

THOMAS. Default credit swaps!

PHILIP. Allahu Akbar!

THOMAS. Participation papers!

PHILIP. Hezbollah!

THOMAS. Certificates!

PHILIP. Jihad!

Their singsong breaks off. Hysterical laughter. Exhausted silence. Pause.

PHILIP. English as a foreign language. How are your private lessons with the commandant coming on?

THOMAS. He's absolutely determined to go to England. Apply for asylum. He'll never make it. (*Imitating him*) 'How are you today?' 'Very well, thank you.' 'Have you sleeped well?'— 'How often do I have to tell you? It isn't *sleeped*—it's *slept*.' 'Have you slept well?' 'Yes.' 'How do you like it here?' 'I like it very much.'

PHILIP. He's making progress.

THOMAS. Enough to drive you mad.

PHILIP. We've had all that before.

THOMAS. We've had all that once before.

PHILIP. Your pills, Thomas. I'm afraid it's the last dose.

THOMAS. Thanks. And what's that there? In the little tube?

PHILIP. Oh that . . . It's my iron ration. Just in case. It would be enough. Have you never thought of that?

THOMAS. End it all? No. Why?

PHILIP. It would be a kind of solution.

THOMAS. Definitely not. It'd be impolite anyway.

PHILIP. Impolite? To whom?

THOMAS. To myself.

PHILIP. A pretty weak argument.

THOMAS. Give me the stuff now.

PHILIP. They're my pills.

THOMAS. I know you and your tricks. They're just placebos.

PHILIP. Of course. Would you like to try one? Be my guest.

THOMAS. Give it to me.

He takes the glass tube and stamps on it and crushes it.

PHILIP. Pity. But you were right, it was only aspirin. (*Pause.*) But you wanted me to amuse you, didn't you? So there you are.

THOMAS. So nothing's going to happen to us any more.

PHILIP. I'm afraid so. (*Pause.*) A beer?

THOMAS. If there's still one left.

They drink.

THOMAS. Warm.

PHILIP. Always the same.

THOMAS. Inevitably. Repetition is reality, the serious side of existence.

PHILIP. What d'you mean?

THOMAS. Insofar as an individual repeats himself as an existing individual by constantly reappropriating his past.

PHILIP. Nonsense.

THOMAS. Kierkegaard.

PHILIP (*laughs*). Oh, in that case . . . Something occurs to me, do you know the one about the Chinaman who goes to Copenhagen and wants to go to the cemetery?

THOMAS. Not again!

PHILIP. Well this Chinaman sees two Danes and asks them, 'Can you tell me the way to the cemetery, please?' The Danes shrug their shoulders because they don't understand Chinese. So the Chinaman tries in English. No reaction. He asks in French, in Russian, in Italian. Again no reaction. The Chinaman gives up and goes away. No cemetery in sight at all. The two Danes look at each other. One says, 'My God, what an educated man.'—'True,' the other says, 'but did it get him anywhere?'

THOMAS (*mocking*). Ha, ha, ha.

PHILIP. Or the one about the man from Hamburg in the desert?

THOMAS. Please, no. I know that one off by heart.

PHILIP. In that case I won't bother. (*Pause.*)

THOMAS. If anyone could hear us. . . . Perhaps we're going out of our minds.

PHILIP. You perhaps, Thomas. I'm perfectly clear-headed.

THOMAS. Any psychiatrist would have us confined to the loony asylum.

PHILIP. We already are.

THOMAS. We are who we are.

It starts to rain again. The light is fading.

THOMAS. This is hell.

PHILIP. Nonsense. Hell is outside. We're in Limbo.

THOMAS. Limbo?

PHILIP. Isn't that in your Kierkegaard? Oh, he was a Protestant, of course.

THOMAS. What are you getting at?

PHILIP. There was a guy in our Jesuit college who was always talking about Limbo. He probably reckoned he was going to end up there himself. An odd fellow. Called Father Ambrosius. Unforgettable. (*Intoning like a Jesuit priest.*) 'Limbo—by some also called the border of Hell, a completely wrong, misleading expression—Limbo is the place where those of the dead stay who have been accorded neither salvation nor damnation.' Got it?

THOMAS. No.

PHILIP. Don't pretend to be more stupid than you are. This camp here—you couldn't call it salvation, but damnation? We shouldn't exaggerate. Death has both advantages and disadvantages, surely you'll allow that. And what do we have? Only the advantages. Or have I got that wrong?

THOMAS. Well at least it's better than out there.

PHILIP. There! You see.

THOMAS. So what?

PHILIP. We're well off here.

THOMAS. Yes, we're well off.

Total darkness. Only the sound of the rain can be heard. The end.

Never has a play of mine flopped with such aplomb! For a few years the Salzburg Festival was in the habit of inviting a 'guest writer'. They were given a small budget from which they were to put on a kind of niche programme in which they would present, among other things, one or two of their own works. Thus in the summer of 1999 it came to a memorable world premiere. It took place in an elegant lodge in the park of a castle, an absurd setting for the two men waiting for death in their shack. A few dozen invited guests, mostly notables who listened politely, attended this private performance.

That same year Roswitha Quadflieg brought out the text with her own illustrations in 250 numbered copies from her Raamin Press: hand-set and printed on Chinese paper by Haag-Drugulin, Leipzig, handbound by Christian Zwang in Hamburg. Never have I been granted a more opulent, exclusive and expensive publication and never was the exclusion of the general public a better-kept secret.

Jacques and His Master

One day André Heller asked me whether I fancied writing something for Gerd Voss. That actor can do anything. His presence alone can fill a large stage. He can be seen as a force of nature. Everyone's a little afraid of him. André claimed he'd like to direct a one-man show for the actor and take it on tour. That would allow Voss to give free rein to his full power without having to bother about losses, colleagues, schedules, and artistic directors. All he needed was a draft, he said, and when they discussed it he'd said he'd like me to do it.

I immediately thought of Denis Diderot who is one of my household gods. To be more precise: his sprawling, witty, lively novel *Jacques and His Master*. Voss knew it and was willing to have a go at it. Now this book consists mainly of dialogues and it's not just two people—the master and his servant—but dozens of voices that tell each other stories, argue, philosophize and lie in a precisely calculated structure. How could a single performer deal with this wide variety? He would have to take on a dozen roles, be master and servant, captain and marquise, innkeeper's wife and police officer at the same time. Only a virtuoso would be up to it.

And it was out of the question just to have a brilliant reader sitting there on a chair entertaining the public as a ventriloquist. He would have to move, take over the whole stage, using all his skill to act out the motivation of all these characters. As Jacques he could give his master, who remains unseen, a piggyback; as master scold his servant, as if he were in the prompt box; a hundred tricks allowing him to quarrel with people, as if they were lurking backstage, in the audience or in the wings.

Both Voss and Heller seemed very taken with my first version, I was the only one who didn't like it. Nor was I happy with a second attempt. But it was enough to plan a tour that was to begin in the provinces and end in the Vienna Burgtheater, where Voss was king.

The project ended when Voss managed to break a leg. It is not without reason that theatre folk are superstitious. A forgotten cable, a treacherous ladder, a short circuit, a loose backdrop and you were calling the doctor. And that's what happened to Gerd Voss one day. And why is it that we bring the story of Jacques and his master to an end with this unfortunate scene?

Simply because, as Jacques the Fatalist says, it is written in the stars—and thus the will of God.

Publishing Projects
That Came to Nothing

Gulliver

Here I could come up with an extensive selection of examples, but I'll content myself with just four. Not all of those reached the threshold of visibility. That is the case with the following project.

The Federal Republic of Germany that we are familiar with was founded at the beginning of the Sixties. Before that we lived in a politically and intellectually backward, provincial protectorate, in which all our energies were directed at patching up the ruined country, at first in a makeshift way, then from top to bottom. At least that's the impression we had back then: we—that is a few people of no consequence who set themselves up as critics of the conditions without anyone asking them to.

In the autumn of 1961, a few of these malcontents had the idea of setting up a magazine. It was to be called *Hallelujah* and was to avoid 'everything boringly tasteful, puritanical, emphatically serious . . . there is no reason to leave politics to the writers of leading articles, reporting to reporters, every field to the relevant specialists . . . fiction and non-fiction will appear beside each other on equal terms, a new poem beside the analysis of a new model of car, an essay on advertising for medicines beside a radio play . . . houses, cycle races, supermarkets, industrial firms, kinds of cheese, professors, tv stars, in brief reality, will be reviewed in the way that until now was reserved for novels. Sections: *antenna*—constant observation of TV-programmes (including those of east germany!); *kiosk*—reports on the german press, ownership, editorial practice; one column is to be reserved for articles rejected by the major german newspapers; an *idiot's column* consisting solely of quotations; view from abroad—german things seen by foreigners, etc.' (It was clearly also to dispense with the capital letters that are such a distinguishing feature of german.)

One of our ambitions with this magazine was to break out of the isolation in which we found ourselves—'with time an international *équipe* is to gather the german core that will follow similar goals. In the initial stages that will come through the observation and utilization of international journals (*express, new statesman, observer, temps modernes, france observateur, the new yorker, evergreen review, vindrosen*, etc.). later this exchange of articles is to evolve into a network of international correspondents.'

The usual suspects were among those involved in this project: Uwe Johnson, Ingeborg Bachmann, Martin Walser, Günter Grass and I. Willy Fleckhaus was to see to the layout, cover and typography. Production, costing, distribution—all that had been described in detail, even obtaining adverts had not been forgotten. We were talking of ten issues per year. The first number never appeared, and no one ever heard about a magazine called *Hallelujah* again.

Perhaps the Federal Republic was simply too small for such ideas? We would have been making some progress, we thought, if we could manage to stake out common ground with kindred spirits from two neighbouring countries. It was France and Italy that we had in mind because we already knew a lot of writers and publishers there. Thus we embarked on a new adventure. Looking back, the list of those who at that time were, more or less definitely, ready to support an international periodical, is quite impressive:

- Ingeborg Bachmann, Uwe Johnson, Martin Walser, Helmut Heissenbüttel, Walter Boehlich, Peter Rühmkorf from Germany and Austria;

- Michel Butor, Roland Barthes, Maurice Blanchot, Michel Leiris, Jean Starobinski, Jean Genet, Marguerite Duras and Maurice Nadeau from France and Switzerland;

- Calvino, Elio Vittorini, Pier Paolo Pasolini, Franco Fortini, Alberto Moravia and Francesco Leonetti from Italy.

Nor was there any lack of publishers who fancied a project like that. Though no firm agreements were made, there were negotiations with Suhrkamp, S. Fischer, Wagenbach and Augstein in Germany; Gallimard and Juillard in France; and

Einaudi and Feltrinelli in Italy. With an alternating group of those involved it looked as if we could have the basis for a bi-monthly magazine.

Over the next two years the aforementioned partners in crime met in Paris, in Zurich, on Majorca and on Corfu in order to press ahead with the project. That cost time and money. All arrangements had to be made by letter since the electronic media were still a long way off. I fear that our painstaking correspondence will have amounted to thousands of pages. Anyone who wonders today what those involved at the time thought they were doing will find themselves faced with a mystery. That is particularly true of the few who were prepared to take on the organization of the three groups themselves. On the German side it was, above all, Uwe Johnson who, with heroic precision, tried to thin out the jungle of hindrances, opinions, interjections, complaints, positive and negative replies. That, as soon will be clear, was a never-ending task. The authors played coy, were hesitant about supplying suitable articles and made countless political or stylistic objections. The publishers were worried about the unforeseeable costs and refused to commit themselves. We couldn't even agree on the title of the publication. New suggestions kept on popping up: *Discorsi, Work in Progress, Rubrik Zeitgeist, Delta, Alea* . . . The working title that proved to be the most popular was 'Gulliver' but even for that there was a vociferous minority that refused to accept it.

Much more serious was the fact that the French group put forward very precise and idiosyncratic ideas regarding the method, the literary forms and structure of the magazine; what they had in mind was clearly the wild notion of an *écriture collective* which was simply not to the taste of the Germans, who were more interested in solid contributions to social and political discourse. At that time people weren't yet talking about the 'death of literature', and even the findings of a few Parisian theorists of literature, who had come to the conclusion that the author was dead, while they were still in the best of health, only reached us with the usual delay at the end of the Eighties.

The first signs of weariness had already appeared after one year. In October 1962, Uwe Johnson was forced to admit that all those involved were showing a clear lack of belief regarding the establishment and survival prospects of the international magazine. One month later I had to report to Germany from Rome that 'gallimard has refused to give the required guarantees. it is not a definitive rejection of the idea, but they were very dubious whether an agreement could be reached. the likelihood is therefore that after two years of "groundwork" the french would be left without a publisher. (which also explained their insistence on paris being the place where meetings would be held. my interpretation is: they haven't a soul.) that means that everything else i could report is of little consequence . . . after what i've learnt in paris it seems as if all that remains is to give the project a decent burial.'

This prognosis turned out to be premature. Despite all the disagreements and sensitivities there was no lack of good will on all sides so the experimental set-up went on for quite a while with a stream of discussions, memoranda, conferences and negotiations. Despite all this, in 1963, Uwe Johnson came to the following conclusion: 'As can be seen from closer examination of the French manuscripts and the translators' reports, they are probably not of a kind that German publishers feel are suitable for German readers. This also applies to a certain extent to the Italian manuscripts as well.'

At that it was probably not only the German group that lost its enthusiasm for *Gulliver*. Presumably we will never be able to establish who, on this journey of discovery, were the giants and who the Lilliputians. At the time I suspected that all concerned were of average height, and made the effort to write a kind of conclusion to the project—a circular of 15 May 1963 that went to all concerned from Tjøme in Norway:

for the moment our project of an international magazine has fallen through. comments on this might seem superfluous, especially when they come from an ex-member of an ex-group, who does not have a particular role as editor of spokesman. i would nevertheless like to say something about the result of our labours . . . because i can only accept the failure of our enterprise on the condition that at least the reasons for and consequences of it are brought out into the open as precisely as possible . . .

the criticism of the articles, the 'ideology' and the composition of the french group by the german 'delegates' seems to me to be largely justified. there would be little point in going into nuances and divergences, my voice would not change the end result at all. however, i see this criticism as an entirely secondary matter, and regret that it clearly became the main topic of the discussions in paris. any criticism of the results of our work ought to be of the total concept we started out with for our magazine. i have looked through the material from that point of view and, therefore, i regard it as unpublishable. and this judgement should not, i think, be restricted to the french contributions, they are just an example. the inadequacy is general, an analogous criticism of details, with similarly devastating results, could just as well be made of the italian and german contributions . . . here too such objections would not be sufficient, not radical, here too it would be a matter of repairs to the surface, of the discussion of symptoms flowing into a delta of trains of thought which lead in different directions the longer you pursue them, just like the paris discussions . . . the first number did not fail because of individual specifiable deficiencies but from its total incoherence: because the individual pieces (both good and bad) do not add up to a clear whole, do not reveal what the point of gathering them together might be. no cosmetic touches and no change of the components can remedy this radical deficiency . . .

the project was set up on the following premises:

1. that among writers from three (perhaps more) countries far-reaching agreement on political questions and on the possibilities of their styles of writing existed or was attainable; that a new method of publication was required and would be sufficient to make this latent understanding productive.

2. that on the basis of these mutual possibilities and intentions the mutual international planning and editing of a magazine was possible.

3. that the contributions for such a magazine would thus allow the creation of such a solid context that an identical publication in three languages was possible.

the result seems to tell me: not that there are better and worse writers among us (that would be nothing new) but that the premises are wrong. that is not to say they are not desirable. their sole disadvantage seems to be that reality nowhere matches up to them . . .

the planning of gulliver was a *coup de force*, an attempt to make things happen *à presque tout prix*, and the result shows that this *coup de force* was unable to change the real situation . . .

like all administrative measures taken 'from above' to impose utopian plans on reality, the idea of the magazine has so far led to an absurd expansion of the technical apparatus, which (like the planning apparatus in some socialist countries) bore no meaningful relationship to the productivity of the system. the amount of correspondence and photocopies, the sheer cost of administration and coordination were a nightmare for me.

I suggested a different procedure instead: gradual, informal collaboration, based on voluntary exchange of material, between three independent magazines. Such a solution would get rid of the 'bureaucratic tendencies and UNESCO-like conference atmosphere at one blow.' For this the necessary starting points were already in existence in France and Italy: Nadeau's *Lettres nouvelles* and Vittorini's *Il menabò*. A suitable magazine was not yet available in Germany but that could change.

In that way I tried to save what could be saved. To do that, however, it seemed to me that first of all the mess that had arisen had to be cleared away: 'i am (for the reasons given) convinced that there are objective reasons for our failure. it would not be appropriate to look for "guilty parties", either individuals or groups. i think that all (almost all, many, some) of those involved have done everything possible, not least the french. maurice blanchot, dionys mascolo and maurice nadeau have, like leonetti and uwe johnson, made considerable sacrifices for this project, sacrifices of time, "professional" sacrifices in one case even physical sacrifices. the same cannot be said of all of those who are criticizing them today . . . if we cannot manage to salvage a minimum of solidarity out of the disaster, then any future attempt to create a new magazine, including the one sketched out here, is doomed to failure. *sine praesumptione sed amice dixi. valete!*'

So all in all *Gulliver*'s interment took place without any shrill disruption. The Italians even gave it a little memorial. Vittorini and Calvino devoted an issue of *Il menabò* to it, that was published in 1964 by Einaudi in Turin.

Our heroic but chaotic test runs had one further consequence. The quarterly, *Kursbuch*, owes its origin to the frustration resulting from this adventure. After more than a year of preparation the first number, edited by myself and Karl Markus Michel, came out with Suhrkamp in June 1965. But that's another story. It would be wrong to tell it here, for it would simply be out of place in a catalogue of failures.

Anyone who is absolutely determined to find out more about the *Gulliver* project will have to consult the following sources:

Elio Vittorini and Italo Calcino (eds), *Il menabò di letteratura 7* (Turin: Einaudi, 1964).

H. M. Enzensberger and Uwe Johnson, *fuer Zwecke der brutalen Verstaendigung. Der Briefwechsel* (Henning Marmulla and Claus Kröger eds) (Frankfurt am Main: Suhrkamp, 2009).

Henning Marmulla, *Enzensbergers Kursbuch* (Berlin: Mattes & Seitz, 2011).

Lignes 11 (Paris, 1990).

Panicali Anna and Maria Chiara Mocali (eds), *Una rivista internazionale mai pubblicata* (Gulliver, 1960–1965). *Testi e correspondeza* (Milan: Bonaparte Quarantotto, 1993); privately printed.

Uwe Johnson and Siegfried Unseld, *Der Briefwechsel* (Eberhard Fahlke and Raimund Fellinger eds) (Frankfurt am Main: Suhrkamp, 1999).

TransAtlantik

So as far as the Seventies are concerned
I can make it brief . . .
By and large they swallowed themselves up
without resisting
did the Seventies,
with no liability assumed
for future generations,
for Turks and the unemployed.
That anyone should remember them fondly
would be asking too much.

So as we were particularly fed up with the spirit of the times we
made a plan, Salvatore and I: one thing among others that we
disliked was that the magazines were full to the brim with gar-
ish photo series on glossy paper and that there was hardly anything to read in them because the captions were written by
people who were not particularly familiar with the German

language. That was another reason why we preferred to read the *New Yorker* that employed all sorts of good writers and went in for a certain elegance. The best thing about that magazine were the well-researched and brilliantly written articles. We did find a certain superciliousness on the part of the editors irritating but we accepted that. Why had something like that been unthinkable in Germany since the Twenties?

There was no question of simply copying our American model, even if the title we'd thought up—*TransAtlantik*—did contain a gentle hint. After all, our little republic wasn't governed from Washington and New York, but from Bonn. Also we didn't necessarily intend to join the scramble for the most prominent authors of the day for our features section but to find new, hungry writers who would be worth considering as reporters. It was also clear to us that bold headlines on the cover were vulgar and that keeping the editorial section in black-and-white was a relief for the eyes. Garishness would be left to the advertising, that had no such inhibitions. In addition it seemed time to improve the taste of the public with a section we would call: 'Journal of Luxury and Fashion'; most people failed to notice that we were referring to a venerable title from Goethe's days. It soon turned out that the bewildered readers saw that announcement as being provocative; back then luxury was flourishing but covertly and was looked on as an abhorrent vice. Even less favourable was the response of many people to the title we had chosen—how could we call our magazine *TransAtlantik* while brave fighters for peace were demonstrating on Mutlanger

Heath against the stationing of American Pershing II rockets? We had clearly not given that a single thought.

However—what publisher would involve himself in such a project that was so out of tune with the times? We couldn't even dream of the large publishing companies; they were sufficiently preoccupied with imitating themselves. Fortunately at that time my friend, Gaston, was a regular at a Munich pub set up by Charles Schumann, where it was usual to wallow in luxury in the form of expensive malt whiskies and Cuban cigars. There, in Harry's Bar, a publisher held court; he was called Heinz van Nouhuys and had a good reputation in the business, for as editor-in-chief of the pictorial magazine *Quick* he had increased its circulation. Envious colleagues tried to get at him by claiming he was a spy and had worked for both sides in the Cold War. They were shooting themselves in the foot, since that allegation was if anything of advantage to his reputation in the world of illustrated magazines. 'What d'you mean, double agent?' he would cry to his fellow topers. 'If I was, then at least a treble one.'

Towards the end of the dire Seventies, he set up his own publishing company, NewMag, which above all brought out a German version of the French magazine called *Lui*. It turned out to be a success because the indecent but carefully touched-up pictures of young ladies were very much appreciated here as well. How Nouhuys financed his business remained a closely guarded secret. It presumably depended on depreciation accounting that in those days was above all popular with consultants, people in the media and pharmacists. Whatever the case, Nouhuys boasted that he had never handed over one single mark to the taxman.

We were impressed by the unscrupulousness of this swash-buckling businessman. We knew that only a man who would stick at nothing came into question for our enterprise. And indeed, in October 1980, we were able to present the first number to an unwelcoming readership and over the next few years to give them the taste for a few writers they hadn't heard of, for example, Martin Mosebach, Christoph Ransmayr, Irene Dische, Bodo Kirchhoff, Reinald Goetz. We were also able to present a variety of readable articles by Lars Gustafsson, Isaiah Berlin, Jane Kramer, Guillermo Cabrera Infante, Stephen Jay Gould and Joseph Brodsky.

But enough of these minor triumphs that were soon to be followed by a long-drawn-out decline. It was a process that gave us valuable insight into the cut-throat business at the newsagent's. Even though we were fortunately not involved in the respective negotiations, we acquired much knowledge about the cunning manipulation of circulation figures, wholesale dis-tribution and advertising agencies. Now and then we also heard about hazardous balancing acts necessary while flirting with real or imaginary investors. To put it briefly: the better the mag-azine looked, the more the number of copies sold declined. After two and a half years we bowed out with no hard feelings but without waiting for the final collapse. There are people who say that *TransAtlantik* failed because it was ahead of its time. That may well have been the case, for life also punishes those who are ahead of their time.

The Intelligencer

I don't know what got into us, but once the long decline and eventual demise of *TransAtlantik* had become inevitable we could think of nothing better than to get down to our next magazine project. This time it was, above all, Karl Markus Michel, Manfred Naber, Tilman Spengler and I who were determined to bestow a further journal alongside *Kursbuch* on the Federal Republic.

This idea also had a precursor. A yellowing piece of paper from 1972 describes a journal for critical science and scientific criticism that was to be called *Index* and that never came to anything. A fictitious first number was to deal with the following topics: socialization and economy; learning processes among primates; syntax and morality; boundary issues in genetics. For 1972 that wasn't that bad. Back then Karl Markus Michel and I had the *New York Review of Books* as a model in mind, that had started during a newspaper strike in 1963 and developed into the main medium of the North American intelligentsia. We told ourselves: Great Britain has not only the traditional *Times Literary Supplement* but also the *London Review of Books*, in Paris there's *La Quinzaine littéraire* and its rivals; *Sinn und Form* is still published in the GDR and even the Soviet Union can afford to have its *Literaturnaya Gazeta*. Why don't we have something like that here?

Michel, who went most deeply into this question, presented us with a new memorandum in June 1981. In it he said, 'Germany is the only developed country in the West to have no standard journal for criticism. The reason that is given for this is also its consequence: the lack of a critical public. To resign in the face of this state of affairs is to be happy to leave scientific and literary life in Germany with the provincial attitude that saves many of its representatives from having to measure their mediocrity by international standards. We do *not* intend to resign, *nor* to remain happy with this.

No one is happy with the state of scientific and literary criticism. Everywhere you can hear the same complaints: it's diffuse, narrow-minded, know-all, ignorant, introspective or short-winded; it's closer to advertising and fashion than to its subjects; it's lacking in rigour, competence and authority . . . People occasionally maintain that over here the science pages or the arts section of the dailies and of some weeklies make up for this to a certain extent . . . But those are 'supplements', add-ons, not autonomous publications, and in order to be seen as topical, they all deal with the same small number of books at the same time. What most commonly comes out of this are book reviews by professional reviewers who, with no regard to their knowledge, pretend to universal competence (and have to do so, since it is how they make their living.)

Michel quoted from 1819/1820 essay by G. W. F. Hegel: *Über die Einrichtung einer kritischen Zeitschrift* (On the Establishment of a Critical Review) as a reminder of a disrupted tradition. In it the philosopher rails against the 'reviewing factories in which mediocrities cosset each other, conferring acclaim and fame' and where 'the habit of passing judgement on the one hand and, on the other, the perennial awareness of passing judgement lead the deluded and the arrogant to the general conviction of being able to produce something at least as good as, if not better than the others, with the result that one could well regard this mutual cultivation of mediocrity, as well as the constant disparagement, as the manure that makes this mediocrity grow ad infinitum.'

Back then we puzzled over what we could do about this. Simple copying the above-mentioned foreign titles would not be enough. Over the months we collected a whole stack of more or less original suggestions: the gaps between the individual academic cultures, people said, should not be filled in but made bridgeable; if an article by an art historian went beyond the mere recounting of content then it would also be of interest to chemists, engineers, linguists, men of the theatre. Research and cultural policy were also key subjects. A regular column on 'translations from academic language into normal German' was also deemed desirable. The virtues of both informative articles dealing with a range of related books and brief polemical reviews should be revived. Novels should not always be reviewed by specialists in literature but, as the case arose, by people who were familiar with the milieu they were set in. In the same way a theatre critic could review an important debate in the Bundestag, an advertising copywriter could write on a volume of poems or a poet could analyse an advertising campaign, etc. Whenever ambitious declarations reached the nadir of embarrassment, for example in government statements, official speeches or TV comments they should be gone over with a fine tooth comb. And, finally, everyone who had been attacked in the magazine should be given the opportunity to fight back, just as the critic should have the right of reply. Such controversies, if they were pursued with no holds barred and in comprehensible German, would perhaps not be without influence on standards operating here.

Strong words! Good intentions! But it didn't stop at declarations about editorial policy. What should *The Intelligencer* look like? Like a 48-page newspaper in half-Berliner format. How often should it appear? Monthly, with a summer break in July and August, that is ten issues per year. How much should it cost?—5 DM per copy; 50 DM for a year's subscription.

We didn't intend to go ahead with the project in amateur fashion, there was a certain amount of publishing and editorial experience in place and there were also people who knew something about typography, production and distribution. Then we had to set up a company of our own. Businessmen, lawyers and tax consultants were questioned. A lot of paper went into calculating the break-even circulation, the fixed, pre-production and variable costs and the proceeds. The result was that *The Intelligencer* would break even with sales of about 25,000 copies.

But where was the initial capital to come from? The project team themselves could chip in the first couple of hundred thousand from their investments in *Kursbuch*, a woman friend promised a further 100,000 DM. So we were at least 900,000 DM short. Sponsors? Patrons? Sleeping partners? Long-term interest-free loans? Allocation of losses for tax purposes? Here fundraisers and specialists in finding grants were needed and it soon turned out that these skills were not our strength.

Perhaps our *Intelligencer* would have failed from its problems with finance anyway, but the actual crux lay elsewhere. It was unforgivable that it was very late before the truth about our intended readership dawned on us. In 1982, there were almost 40,000 university professors in Germany, Austria and Switzerland and every year almost 100,000 students graduated from the universities. We can only guess at the size of the academic labour market in industry, in research institutes and in the media. At the beginning of the Eighties, almost all these people could still count on getting what is called a steady job. That was nice but, unlike in the USA, considerably reduced the competition for positions.

The success of the *New York Review of Books* was not solely based on the quality of its writing but also on the harsh conditions governing the intellectual labour market in the States. Anyone who doesn't keep up and isn't prepared to invest time and money in continuing their professional training will find the cards stacked against them. Unfortunately, what the group in Berlin trying to set up a journal didn't realize was that things were quite different in Germany. If a German professor, editor, scientist or theatre director read such a magazine at all, then they would at best leaf through their department library's, their firm's or their office's copy. The idea of taking out and paying for a personal subscription would never occur to them. Thus the little team of dreamers who didn't take account of this well-known fact had no one but themselves to blame for the failure of their project.

The Frankfurter Allgemeine Library

It is a miracle that things went well for 20 years, that I had a free hand, that two firms just let me get on with it and that in those two decades more than 250 volumes of the *Andere Biblio-thek* (The Other Library) could be published. There is a clear message in the saying, 'He who pays the piper calls the tune', only it didn't apply to me. I had a free hand, and what was even better: I didn't have to go into the office and could play at being editor and publisher at home. This ideal situation was only pos-sible because of Greno in Nördlingen and Eichborn in Frank-furt. No big publisher would have touched such a project with a bargepole.

It was a classic case of informal but close self-organization: a writer, a printer, typographer and book designer such as Greno, who was master of his own workshop, an irreplaceable typesetter such as Schmidberger, a bookbinder such as Lachen-maier in Reutlingen, publishers such as Vito von Eichborn and

Uwe Gruhle, editors such as Reinhard Kaiser and Rainer Wieland —without them and many others, who saw to the infrastructure, the *Andere Bibliothek* would never have made it out of the starting blocks.

I'm afraid we never earned a decent return but we did manage to keep out of the red by the skin of our teeth. Subventions mostly makes people stupid; constant underfunding endangers your independence or, to put it briefly, there's no such thing as a free lunch.

There's no point in assuming the role of narrator here and describing the many vicissitudes we survived. The sole matter of relevance is the parting of the ways in which it ended. It followed the usual rules, which so far we'd ignored with impunity. It began with the transformation of Eichborn Ltd into a public limited company and with a flotation. It's difficult to say who first pulled the ripcord, nor is it of any importance. Let us not call what came to a head then a row, let's call it material fatigue. Anyway, in October 2004 I handed in my notice as consulting editor with Eichborn with effect from the following March. Anyone who knows lawyers, however, will be well aware that something like that can drag on.

Now you might think that after 20 years I'd have had enough of the publishing business. And indeed, I did have the feeling that the little drama in Frankfurt had done me good; it was, as they say in English, a blessing in disguise.

Then something remarkable happened. Suddenly people arrived who had been observing our team and thought they could make some use of us. One was Frank Schirrmacher, an editor of the *Frankfurter Allgemeine Zeitung*; the other was Wolfgang Balk, who today is still the head of the very successful Deutscher Taschenbuch Verlag (dtv) in Munich. The two of them suggested a cooperative enterprise such as had never existed before. (That dailies should open shops of their own and sell books and music, bottles of wine and films was not the rule back then.)

Greno, a man who enjoyed small-scale projects, was immediately hooked. In next to no time he was developing maquettes, illustrations, advertising material and samples of typesetting. Even today I still have a few copies of his magnificent dummy books. There was agreement that the new series of books should be called the *Frankfurter Allgemeine Library*.

I have to admit that I wasn't as keen on it as Greno. The programme was the least of my worries—I had always kept a long list of possible titles. And there would be no lack of authors, translators, editors and scouts. In April 2005 a contract was already there on the table. However it took countless meetings to sort out the details, in which, as is well known, the devil resides, and if there's something I find hard to bear, it's meetings.

The bigger an institution, the more detours are necessary to come to a decision. We, of course, were gnomes compared with the *Frankfurter Allgemeine Zeitung*. Moreover we had no idea of the internal problems such a large enterprise had to contend with. Our sponsor in the Frankfurt firm, Frank Schirrmacher, was based in one of two high-rise buildings in Hellerhofstrasse. There the editors, who know how to defend their rights and privileges, have their offices with all their staff. In the tower opposite are the members of the supervisory board, the executives, the managers of the distribution, marketing and advertising departments and other important persons who see to it that enough money is earned to keep the editorial office going. Very high up there's a glass bridge between the two buildings but very little use is made of it, which is presumably the result of the interesting dynamics between the two pillars of the business. We had the impression that one side saw control freaks and bean-counters on the other, while conversely they thought they were dealing with prima donnas and quibblers. What kept the two factions together was the conviction that they had been chosen to guard a holy grail called the *FAZ*, three initials that all the company cars displayed.

Greno and I were frequently summoned by the management; a special conference was arranged in Berlin to discuss a planned poster. Our project was also the subject of exhaustive discussions at dtv and Wolfgang Balk left us in no doubt that he would make it his baby.

The *Frankfurter Allgemeine Bibliothek* was to make its debut at the autumn 2005 Book Fair with its first six titles. Among these were: a new novel by Irene Dische, a large-scale report by Matthias Matussek (*Palasthotel. Wie die Einheit über Deutschland hereinbrach*—Palace Hotel. How Unity Befell the Germans), a German translation of Arthur Koestler's *The Sleepwalkers*,

Astolphe de Custine's clairvoyant letters from Russia in 1839: *Russische Schatten* (Russian Shadows) with an essay by Sonja Margolina, and other nice things.

Greno had already presented a brochure that was to be included in the newspaper. The representatives of dtv were supplied with specimen copies, a programme of future editions and sales strategies. It would be ridiculous, they said in one voice, if two such powerful players as these two elephants couldn't make a splash the industry would remember for a long time.

But it never came to that. One day Eichborn sought an injunction from the Frankfurt am Main regional court to prevent Greno and myself from doing what we proposed.

That was the beginning of a pretty long affair that dragged on over many months and was as expensive as tedious for all concerned. Files were filled with writs, demands for compensation, requests for a declaratory judgement and counterclaims. In the initial hearing the regional court came down on our side. Subsequently, however, the regional high court, taking the subtle technicalities of competition law into account, came to the opposite conclusion, forbade us to go ahead and threatened us, should we continue, with a fine of up to €250,000 or a term in prison of up to six months. The *Frankfurter Allgemeine* informed up in three laconic lines that the contract between us had become (was therefore) frustrated and even that brave soul Wolfgang Balk had, though unwillingly, to withdraw. The wrangling with Eichborn ended six months later, when everyone involved had become tired of it, with a settlement. Alexander

Kluge told me he had never acted for himself in court and he should know what he's talking about as he is a lawyer himself. There was another valuable lesson we learnt from our little mammoth project: the greater the undertaking, the more noise it makes when it comes to nothing. Anyone who would like to complain about this should follow the advice of an old Saxon poet, who had to deal with less innocuous hardships: 'Be thou yet undaunted. Give nothing up for lost.'

My Literary Projects
That Came to Nothing

Children and Money

Even as an author, some of my projects have come to nothing. I'm not talking here about the number of copies sold or reviewers who weren't well-disposed towards me. As far as those of my books are concerned which, as the publishers' royalty payments indicate, are blooming unseen, I see no reason to complain, never mind feel regret—I still feel as attached to most of these lost children as ever. The only one who suffers from them is the publisher, whose business they are spoiling; the author, on the other hand, loves these luxurious products. Anyone who has their bank account in mind while writing a book is already lost.

No, true failure for an author appears on a quite different, invisible list, the one containing their abandoned books. I am reluctant to reveal what my changelings and bastards were about and why they never saw the light of day. One example must suffice here.

I have long been annoyed that there are matters that are neglected in our schools but that we are all confronted with at some time or other, for example the law. The consequence is that most people are terrified when a lawyer's letter flutters in through their letter box or, what is worse, when it is a matter of a 'submission'. ('If it is not possible for the submission to be delivered according to ¶173 Sect.1 No. 3 or ¶180, the document in question can be deposited in the offices of the court of the administrative district in which the place of delivery lies. A written communication regarding such a deposition, made on the form provided under the address of the person to whom it is to be delivered, is to be sent in the usual way for ordinary letters or, if that is not possible, attached to the door of the apartment, the offices or the community facility. Once the written communication has been thus handed over, the document is regarded as delivered.') The average citizen is helpless when faced with such outrageous gobbledegook.

But that is far from being everything that is lacking in our overextended school system. Most things connected with money are also more or less taboo in lessons. I suspect that this is connected with the personal financial situation of the teachers who, as is well known, are on permanent contracts and don't have to waste time wondering about their salaries and pensions. At most the pupils are told about the negative side-effects of capitalism but right up to the school-leaving exam not much is said about currency questions, the balance of payments, market rates, economic cycles, capital markets and suchlike. And that when not only most of the grown-ups' conversations are about dough, but their children too are eagerly looking forward to the next installment of pocket money, searching the internet for special offers and involved in lively barter trade.

Perhaps it's about time, I thought, to do something about the schools' meagre offerings in this respect and offer the 12- to 17-year-olds, who suffer from it, a little training programme; and that not in the form of a textbook—textbooks are the last things they're short of—but as a story in which everything crops up that is missing from their timetable, in a word, the economy. The story wasn't to be like the usual compulsory reading but exciting, amusing and a little mischievous.

That can't be all that difficult, I thought, and roughed out a kind of novel in which an old money-forger, a young woman involved in speculation, a miser and a spendthrift appeared. But after about 150 pages and a chaotic dossier full of ideas, I gave up for the time being.

My subject turned out to be so vast that no narrative vehicle could accommodate such an immense load. The ruins of this monstrosity of a project can be viewed on my hard disc, the *disjecta membra* of a bestseller with which, as with so many other things, I have so far not burdened the world. Though I can't promise that it will stay that way. It is, after all, a piece of work for which I am not dependent on the goodwill of directors, producers or administrators—an attraction that only literature has to offer.

In fact the best strategy of all is probably to do what you happen to feel like doing.

Below is a short extract from the first chapter of a book, that had the working title of *Children and Money*:

I can remember very well how innocuous the beginnings of this crazy story were. It was a quite ordinary Friday evening, a week before the summer holidays began, in that tacky corner pub that was called, of all things, Tivoli. That was where our crowd used to meet: Robert, Mimi, Niklas, Schlock (he was actually called Christian but no one called him that) and me, of course, Eliza whom everyone, God knows why, called Shrew.

Actually we didn't really belong together. Our gang of five was, I believe, nothing but an alliance of outsiders who had got together for want of anything better. Each one of us was an only child and we were bored at home. We stuck together for years simply because the others in the class were even more stupid. The only sensible one was probably Robert, although he had all sorts of quirks, for example his secretiveness, with which he kept getting on our nerves. Not to mention Niklas, the puritan. He was always going on at us about his obsessions, his pangs of conscience, as if the world were simply waiting for him to improve it. He was consistent, you have to give him that. He had run away from home, because his old man had something to do with atomic power stations, and found refuge in a commune. He was quite the opposite to our *bon viveur*, fat Schlock, a spoilt mummy's boy, who spent money like it was going out of fashion;

everyone fell for his languid charm, even the woman who taught us chemistry; I was the only one he got nowhere with. Then, last but no least, Mimi, the Brazilian. I found her more difficult to resist even though, between ourselves, she was and is something of a slut. Sometimes I envied her, not just because of her fantastic figure and because all the guys were after her but because she was afraid of nothing and, unlike me, wasn't always worrying about something. All in all an unlikely group! But it's a mystery why such cliques exist and how they come together. One day you find you belong and it's too late to get out of it.

So I was always there, on that evening as well, even though I couldn't stand the Tivoli, the suburban pub where there were mostly drunk blue-collar workers and gone-to-seed allotment holders sitting around. God knows who started us going there. It was probably Mimi. She's always been quite happy to spend the night in some flea-ridden dosshouse. She feels just as much at home in any favela as in a five-star hotel. Moreover, the Tivoli was in a dilapidated slum behind the goods yard on the edge of town, only inhabited by the poorest pensioners with their dogs and Pakistani families who hadn't yet made it to a snack bar. It was probably because of all the immigrants that the district was just called 'Iraq'. But despite that the Tivoli was only a few blocks away from the Arizona Hall and that was absolutely the place to be. So since we had to pass the time somewhere or other until things got going there, and that wasn't before 11 in the evening, we would end up in that dreary pub twice a week.

So that Friday we were there again in the murky light of a 40-watt bulb, each with a beer and moaning, as usual, about school. Then Schlock, generous as ever, pulled out a joint and handed it around. Aha, I said, you've enough for that but never when it's a matter of paying your debts.

Schlock always came to me whenever he was broke. I was his bank. Word had got around in the class that I was always ready to oblige. I started doing it purely out of good nature, €50 here, €100 there, and it had never occurred to me to make it a business. But soon I was forced to realize that these kids just kept muddling along with no thought of paying it back in time. Even in the fourth form I was already owed huge sums and I had to write off half of the first two thousand. Things couldn't continue like that, of course, from then on I had to charge interest, otherwise I'd have been stony broke myself. There's practically no security for loans and I was taking an incredibly big risk. I must have been mad to get involved in something like that, it's definitely not a way of making friends. Anyone who refused to pay would call me a bloodsucker and once the father of a boy in the other class reported me to the school authorities. And that guy happened to be a tax adviser who made his money by helping his clients hide their dough from the income tax people.

Anyway, I was annoyed with Schlock, who was in debt to me to the tune of around €800 and always claimed he hadn't a cent. But there was always enough for his black Afghan that he would hand around like nobody's business.

Perhaps I shouldn't have mentioned it, now the whole evening was ruined. They all forgot their stupid stories about school and an argument started that I can still remember today because that's where it all began. Suddenly the group had something to talk about. Schlock was giving me reproachful, not to say furious looks.

'Money, money, money!' he shouted, so loud that the allotment holders' heads shot up. 'I'm sick of hearing about it. Everywhere you go, during break, on the bus, in the cafe it's always the same.'

'You're only getting worked up because Shrew wants her money back,' Robert said.

'Rubbish. She can go and get knotted for all I care. No, it's much worse. The other day I was walking in the park behind a married couple, old-age pensioners. He was limping, she was going on and on at him and she kept on saying bank statement, final demand. 'That Metzinger,' she shrieked, 'he's going to send in the bailiffs.' At this he, her husband, also exasperated, shouted at her, 'Because you're always throwing the money out of the window for your cat food!' It makes no difference whether it's the man begging outside the bank or my old man at dinner, they're all talking about the same thing all the time—money, money, money. Yesterday he was going on about it again. He moans about taxes or he's worried about some shares or other. It's enough to drive you mad. And you lot, you're all the same.'

'Is that you done, Schlock? Come over here, then and have a drink,' Mimi said. 'It's not as bad as all that.'

'Just a minute.' Now it was Niklas, and when Niklas talks it's not that easy to stop him. 'That's just like Schlock. It's easy for him to talk. He's above that kind of thing. Because he's always got enough in his pocket. That's right, isn't it, Schlock? Your mum always makes sure your pockets are full. Go on, show us your credit card. Recently I saw you at the cash machine. And do you know what he said, guys? I've got to release a few hundred for myself. Release! As if the poor money was locked up in there and he has to liberate it.'

'So what?' said Mimi. 'You should be happy that at least Schlock can get a few euros from the bank. I'd be happy if I had something to liberate. We were thinking of going to Portugal in September, have you all forgotten? And now Niklas is talking as if money had nothing to do with it. I'd like to know how he imagines that will be. Even if we sleep in the train, it could well cost each of us a thousand euros. So what do you say? Are we going or aren't we?'

'Of course we're going,' Robert said. 'If necessary we'll borrow the money. What d'you think, Eliza?'

'Oh do stop it,' I said. 'We'll never get anywhere like this. Not one of you has any idea what you're talking about.'

'Really? But of course you know what you're talking about, don't you Shrew?'

Now they all started to go on at me. 'Don't call me Shrew. My name's Eliza. How often do I have to tell you?'

'OK, OK, Shrew. You tell us. You're our specialist, our money expert.'

But I refused to get worked up. If there's one thing I do know: I know when I know about something and when not. Only my dear friends, they had no idea how clueless they were. And there was no surprise in that.

We'd just finished eight years slaving away at high school and what had they drummed into us? Everything, absolutely everything about photosynthesis, the theory of relativity, combinatorics and the Holocaust. But something about money, public spending ratios, capital markets, economic cycles, monetary policy—no chance!

'But what's all that got to do with our trip to Portugal?—Capital markets, don't make me laugh.—Bighead!' they all cried at once. I often get that because I sometimes show off, not bothering what the others think. But I refused to lose my cool.

'Now just you all listen,' I went on. 'Every time you have a problem with money, no matter what it's about, clothes, pocket money or, if you like, our trip to Portugal, you behave like absolute idiots because you've never really thought about it properly. Because you don't want to know. Isn't that so, Schlock? Or because you're simply against it, like good old Niklas. Or because our stuffy school naturally had something better to do than to make you fit of economic life. They fill you full of the biology of amoebas and piano sonatas. I can tell you why our teachers, standing there in front of the class, never talk about money. Because they have no idea about it themselves. I'm aware of all this because my old man's a prime example: nothing but physics and maths for 15 years and for that he has his salary paid into his account every month, and that's that. At most he'll moan a bit at home because it's never enough and because I need some new gym shoes or because we have a mortgage on our house. Otherwise he calmly sits there waiting for his pension. That's not going to happen to me, I can tell you.'

'Of course it's not,' Niklas snapped. 'You're our financial genius. You'd like it best if you could write your leaving exam in a bank.'

'Even that would be better than at our school,' I said, 'where the teachers stuff our heads full of useless rubbish.'

'So what?' Schlock muttered. 'Why shouldn't they? At least they don't bore us to death going on and on about money. Tax assessment, stock market flotation, recession—it's enough to make you sick.'

At last Robert joined in. He's not as narrow-minded as the others, you have to give him that. He always listens to everything, keeps his cool, but when he opens his mouth what he says makes sense.

'Eliza's right,' he said. 'Like it or not, we can't avoid the economy.'

'You two just want to get rich,' Niklas interjected. Niklas was our moralist. Greenpeace, down with globalization, third world campaigns and so on.

'Of course I want to get rich,' I said, just to annoy Niklas, if for no other reason. 'What's wrong with that?'

'That's just like you. I can already see you climbing the ladder, that's all you can think of.'

'That's not what this is all about,' Robert said. 'You of all people, my dear Niklas, would benefit from having a clearer view of these things. How can you attack capitalism if you don't understand how it works?'

'Well I just want to be left in peace and not have to spend all my time wondering what my bank account looks like.' That was Schlock, of course, who just wanted to enjoy life without any ambition at all.

'We'll probably all spend a few years hanging around at university,' I said, 'perhaps with a few vacation jobs. But what then? Surely you don't seriously believe the world is going to roll out the red carpet for us? Anyone who doesn't want to end up on social security will have to do a bit of hard thinking.'

'Oh yes, Shrew, you'll certainly make it: four years of Business Administration, then a year in the States and a few years later you'll end up with a top job in management.'

'That's not for me,' Schlock said.

'Still,' Robert said, 'I can't see why we shouldn't know what's happening in the so-called economy. We don't need experts for that. After all, the guys up in their glass house are no different from the rest of us. It can't be all that much of a mystery. We're not stupid either.'

'So what's the point of all this?' that was Mimi joining in, finally.

'Well,' I said, 'how about meeting in the afternoon for a while to talk about money? A kind of fitness training in economics— instead of your eternal tennis or riding lessons, or you with your Brazilian hip-hop, Mimi.'

'And what's that got to do with Portugal? I can tell you now, I'm going to lie on the beach and go dancing in the evening.'

'If that's what you want, Mimi. But I'll bring the *Financial Times* along and then we can have a bit of a discussion.'

Schlock groaned. 'Now you know—Shrew's gone off her rocker. One more advanced course, that's all I needed.'

'That's just you all over, Eliza,' Niklas said nastily. 'But you watch out. Don't go thinking you'll get us joining in your hymns of praise to capital. There's going to be a real barney about that.'

'All the better,' I said.

'You lot can do as you like,' Mimi said. 'You might as well start with your seminar on money right away. But count me out. Weren't we going to go to the Arizona? It's 11 already. Who's coming?'

My Etcetera Projects
That Came to Nothing

The Fountain of Poetry

There are inventions that are difficult to improve on—for example, the spoon, the bicycle and the book. They don't need defending. They aren't sacred, merely very useful. Books, for example. They don't need a chip, instructions for use, a battery, an aerial, a password, and their operating system is extremely durable; we don't need to upgrade them every few years with new hard- and software.

Despite that language and, therefore, poetry as well, create things that do not fit on a page. The reason is that paper has only two dimensions. So how about a third? For that we'd have to construct objects that make a different use possible. For example: a poetry machine or all kinds of complicated word-toys. I have done that. Such things have been even made and exhibited and now and then people came who took a fancy to them. I had less luck with my *Fountain of Poetry*.

My first proposal for this project came, I believe, in 1998. This was what it was like:

I

'Art for buildings'—the results of such well-meaning campaigns are not always convincing. Just as people in a city can hardly remember whom the massive equestrian statues they hurry past every day represent, they become so familiar with modern sculptures they hardly notice them any more. In a way they become invisible; people walk around them without looking at them. You might almost think they were nothing but obstructions.

So anyone who has the idea of commissioning a work of art that will not only be looked at in the first moment but also in the long run, needs to come up with something new: a fountain of poetry, for example, with a cascade of water in which a new message will appear every day.

II

A film of water will flow down over a sloping glass plate, at least 150 x 90 cm, set at eye-level. The circulation of water can be so arranged that it produces a smoother or more rippling surface, depending on the pressure; when the flow is reduced, individual drops will be seen trickling down, as on a windowpane when it's raining.

Texts will be projected onto the glass plate. The lines will move from the bottom to the top, against the flow of water, not too quickly and not too slowly. The slight turbulence of the water, the formation of drops and trickles, will bring the writing alive, it will quiver a little, some letters will be a touch enlarged while the refraction of light will make others seem brighter than those around. A relatively large type size will be necessary so that the lines are still legible.

As far as the technical aspect is concerned, there is a solution which will not be difficult to implement, given the present state of technology. Plasma and LCD screens are out of the question: they are too much trouble to install and electronics and water don't go well together.

A beamer that projects the text onto the glass plate is not too difficult to install and maintain. These devices are factory-made and have reached a high degree of precision over the last few years. The circulation of water presents no difficulties.

The text will be controlled by a computer that can then transmit the data directly.

If installed in the open air, the incidence of light on the glass plate would create interference; moreover the installation would be open to the elements, therefore, the fountain should be sited in a large internal space, an entrance hall or foyer with subdued lighting.

III

A large supply of text is necessary for the system to have constant new surprises, and that has already been arranged.

The programme will have a running time of at least 180 minutes. If we assume that the average person who is attracted to it will spend five minutes by the fountain, the probability of them coming across the same text at a second visit is very low, in this particular case 1:36—that is, they would only see a repeat at every 36th visit.

The initial body of texts consists of a collection of literary extracts dealing with water in all possible different ways. None should be longer than 8–10 lines and for that reason alone poems are to be preferred because they have the highest degree of concentration: everything is said in a few lines. But in the long run an anthology of poetry could easily become monotonous, therefore aphorisms, nursery rhymes, proverbs, nonsense poems and short pieces from the meteorology, physics and chemistry of water have been included. Occasionally English, perhaps even French, Italian, Spanish or Latin sources may appear. The final collection is to be agreed with the person who commissions it.

Anyway, preference is generally given to texts that, in one way or another, are on the theme of water. Metaphorical usages are also included (time like a stream, tears, thirst, drinking, rain, deluge, etc.). There is a rich tradition but there should be no lack of more recent items, including newspaper articles as far as I'm concerned. The cost of the fountain will be more or less what a sculptor charges for a new work.

No one will find a poetry fountain, that not only exploits the magic of water but has it as a theme, boring; it will offer more variety than any monument. Even casual observers will be enticed into spending some time following the interplay of water and poetry. And every time they come back, there will be something new to see.

Where? That was the next question. An airport departure lounge where the passengers are bored? The foyer of a high-rise building? The head office of a water company? The pump room of a spa? Horst Brandstätter, a friend who was always good for new ideas, had managed to find an investor who was planning, somewhere in Thuringia, one of those monstrous spa health farms that were popping up like mushrooms after the Berlin wall came down. However it soon turned out that the man was a genius at getting subsidies who worked with a complicated system of write-offs. The health paradise was actually built, but the entrepreneur had long since disappeared and our project with him.

Many years later an Iraqi poet organized an excursion to the United Arab Emirates, where she obviously had good connections. The meeting between Arabic and German writers and philosophers took place on the invitation of the sheikh, who bore the impressive name of Mohammed bin Rashid Al Maktoum. 'In the next few years theatres, research and conference centres will be built there and I've been asked to design the world's first poetry museum,' Amal Al Jubouri told me. 'And for that I'll definitely need your fountain. *The Fountain of Poetry.*'

André Heller who, with his *Artevent* organization in Vienna, has all possible kinds of experts at his disposal, was happy to take on the project. An architecture firm he was friendly with supplied detailed plans and estimates of cost. By now the fountain had got bigger and bigger and more and more expensive. It looked like a futuristic monument in a sea of sand.

In November 2009, the Dubai boom had reached its dizzying climax. We were all spoilt beyond measure. The luxury of the hotel was frightening, there were excursions to camel-breeders and hunting with falcons. The emir's brother, who wrote poetry himself, liked my idea. In the desert, he said, water was precious, a magic element, and there would therefore be no problem finding wonderful new and classical Arabic poems on the subject. 'We are definitely going to do it,' he concluded. 'The head of my foundation will see to it and agree a *letter of intent* with you.'

The days simply flew past. A postmodern oriental carpet carried us through bazaars, court ceremonies with speeches emphasizing international unity and diplomats' villas with marble columns. On the day we left only one signature was lacking. We never heard anything further from Sheikh Mohammed bin Rashid. When, a few months later, the first reports of a credit squeeze in the Emirates appeared on the ticker-tape, we realized why. None of my failed projects was so magical and so crazy.

A Help-Yourself Store of Ideas

Most people are born project-makers. We can't stop constantly thinking up new plans, even when our earlier ones have burst like bubbles. Which of us does not have far more ideas flitting through their mind than they can ever realize? This teeming throng is ruled by the laws of development: waste, selection and mutation are the order of the day. Magnificent and stupid, promising and hopeless schemes contest the ground. There is certainly no lack of them and therefore the fear that someone else might steal *my* concept, *my* brilliant project, *my* unique design, is nothing but a symptom of neurosis. There's no copyright on ideas. Should anyone therefore find something useful in the following haystack of abandoned plans—just go ahead. Have fun. In contrast to the case with the proud failures described in the first part of this book, anyone who plunders this store of ideas need have no fear a lawyer might come hammering at their door with a list of demands. A footnote will suffice.

The following ideas have never made it beyond the sketch stage. I am comfortable with that since in that case I have been spared the struggles and disappointments, the defeats and humiliations that are usually associated with the realization of tantalizing plans.

Ideas for Films

The Switch

What actually is a 'pro'? And why is that abbreviated word taken as a compliment? Does it mean that someone has learnt something, a trade, for example, a profession? There would be no objection to that if it didn't evoke echoes of the old adage, cobbler, stick to your last. Why should he, actually? If he'd stuck to that principle, Jakob Böhme would have done better to steer clear of philosophy and to have made a pair of boots instead of writing *Morgenröte im Aufgang* (*Aurora*). It's very boring having to stick, like a waiter, to the area that has been allocated to you. It's much more enjoyable, it seems to me, to go poaching on other people's territory. And, unlike the cobbler from Görlitz, you don't have to produce a masterpiece.

In the 1940s I preferred to go to the cinema rather than, as they said back then, go 'on duty'. It was dark in the cinema and no one noticed that I was wearing the shit-brown uniform of the so-called Hitler Youth. I obviously had no lack of chutzpah;

I remember telling myself: you can do what those film people at UFA do. Thus I would quietly think up completely preposterous films of my own. Fortunately, I didn't wrote them down.

That came much later. Recently I happened upon a long-forgotten, neatly typed manuscript from 1954 in a drawer. Back then I had a little Olivetti typewriter, the one with the red backspace key. I was very proud of my acquisition and, even though I didn't feel I was a 'pro' and had neither money nor the slightest knowledge of the film industry, I set to work. The following is an extract from those yellowing pages:

EXPOSITION

Good fortune has many faces; here it appears in the mask of the chauffeur Lucky, who is a reliable driver but a deceitful and smug angel.

Lucky drives the powerful car of the newspaper magnate Maximilian Röding, who has a serious heart condition. He worries about his work, even in his dreams. He feels sorry for himself; he tyrannizes his staff, especially his secretary, an obstinate bachelor called Schlicke, who practically runs the whole business, while Röding is fighting with the ghosts of his private life. He has married a young, pretty, demanding woman whom he has at first spoilt, then neglected and finally forgotten. This Daniela is now leading an expensive, stupid and sad life, keeping out of the way of Röding. His two children from his first marriage have become strangers to him, even though they live in the house. Mell, 20, is studying archaeology and despises his father because 'his head

is full of nothing but money and politics—filthy stuff, that is.'
Caroline, 17, goes around with low-class artists whom Röding,
probably with some justification, finds outrageous. Also living in
the house is the publisher's mother, a parsimonious and impos-
ing lady, who prefers the way of life of long-gone times.

Röding is afraid because he's ill and alone. He is more and
more haunted by the desire to escape from his existence and
start a new life at 50, a simple life away from the limelight. That,
he believes, is his only chance of reaching old age. He confides
this hope to Lucky, his chauffeur. He sees him as the only person
who can understand his problems.

Röding has a double, whom he knows nothing about, no
more than the other does of him. This man, a farmer called
Maximilian Klamm, lives only a few hundred yards away, though
almost in a different age, in Unklaich, a village on the border. Life
is very hard there. In earlier times the peasants in the barren
wooded area mostly made their living from smuggling. Since the
war the border has been sealed off. Klamm is in a bad way. He is
just as dissatisfied as Röding. His wife, Margarete, is having a
fairly open affair with Anton, the labourer, who has become the
real master of the farm. Klamm is over 50 and suffers from gout.
Worn down by the constant arguing, he's turned to drink. His
daughter Frieda would most of all like to sell the farm. Her dream
is of a hotel on the trunk road that goes past Unklaich. Philomena
Klamm, the farmer's mother, is a harsh, obstinate, sanctimo-
nious bigot.

When Klamm, on his way back from the inn, sees the businessmen's limousines waiting at the customs post he is seized with envious rage at the people from the city. The men in their camel-hair coats stretching their legs at customs don't have gout, he thinks, their wives are young and their children obedient. He'd like to break out of his depressing life in Unklaich.

Klamm and Röding will, of course, be played by the same actor.

PLOT OUTLINE

Röding, driven by Lucky, is on his way back from one of the many foreign journeys his work forces him to take. He is bitter at the thought of returning to his business and his family. He talks to Lucky about this while they're waiting at the border. Full of envy, he watches the Unklaich farmers sitting outside the inn with their glasses of beer. 'This is where I'd like to end my days,' he says. His chauffeur argues against this but can't convince him.

Now Klamm has had another argument with his wife. He threatens to throw her and Anton out. Margarete tells him contemptuously to his face that with his gout he's a semi-cripple and in fact it's Anton who's feeding the whole family. Klamm stamps out of the house in fury, determined to leave the village and start a new life somewhere in the town.

As Lucky is driving off after they've been through customs, Röding shows signs he might be having a heart attack. Lucky stops by the road in the woods, takes off his boss's tie and jacket and helps him out of the car. Röding sits down on a tree trunk.

Once he has got his breath back he says he'd like to take a walk through the forest for a few minutes, until he feels better again.

After a while Klamm appears on the road. Lucky grins when he sees him and asks politely if he wants to drive on now. Klamm hesitates, thinking the chauffeur is making fun of him. But since the unusual invitation comes at the right moment for him, he gets in and Lucky drives on with the false Röding.

The real Röding, still puffing and panting, comes back out of the woods. He rubs his eyes: his car has gone and doesn't come back. At first he's puzzled, then annoyed. Since he's thirsty he goes to the nearest farm and asks for a glass of milk. There Frau Klamm, who has a guilty conscience because of the earlier argument, greets him in friendly fashion by his Christian name. He is even more surprised when she asks him how he comes to be in those ridiculous city clothes. Eventually he realizes she's taken him for someone else. When he tries to explain the mistake, she simply laughs at him. Since he's still exhausted from his heart attack and feels very tired, he gives way and spends the night on the farm. To his relief he sees that Margarete withdraws to the labourer's bedroom so that he can sleep undisturbed. His wife and labourer agree that the farmer has obviously had too much to drink; that, they think, explains his behaviour and the odd things he says.

Meanwhile Lucky has helped the farmer to put on the publisher's jacket, which also contains his wallet. In one last burst of honesty, Klamm tries to protest but Lucky, who is quite clear about the switch, keeps going on at him until he tries on

Röding's camel-hair coat. Now all he needs is a white shirt and a pair of trousers, which Lucky quickly gets once they're in the town. In Röding's office, Klamm finds, to his embarrassment, that he's addressed as boss. That evening in a wine bar Lucky gets him to the point where, though with a shake of his head, he is not unhappy to accept the situation as a dream. That both Klamm and Röding accept their new roles naturally rests on the fact that they correspond to their deepest and most secret desires.

Despite that, when he wakes up under Klamm's eiderdown the next morning Röding decides to put an end to the matter and go into the village to telephone for his car. However, he soon realizes that his jacket, with all his papers and money, was left in the car. The people in the village all greet him as Klamm. Since no one will listen to him and he has no coins, he doesn't manage to reconnect with his earlier life. Back on the farm he is completely taken over by the family who find that, despite the quirky things he comes out with, he has very much changed for the better. Eventually he decides to see his stay in Unklaich as the first real holiday he's had for years. He gloats over the baffled expressions there must be on the faces of those at home and in the office at his absence. Moreover he assumes this can't last for long; Lucky will certainly come to find him and clear up all the misunderstandings.

Late that evening Lucky drives up to Röding's house with his protégé. The villa and the family, especially the attractive Daniela, make a great impression on Klamm. With his innate cunning he

207 |IDEAS FOR FILMS

tries to accustom himself to his new role. Lucky skilfully deals with awkward situations. The family are pleasantly surprised at the rustic charm of their lord and master and his unaccustomed obliging ways. They come to the conclusion that he has made a splendid recovery during the trip. Only the old lady is horrified at the lack of manners he suddenly displays.

Both of the men involved in the switch get more and more caught up in their alien lives. Klamm becomes familiar with the trials of a manager, Röding with those of a farmer. As Lucky has made clear to him, the new boss approves of everything that is put before him and signs documents laboriously but accurately with Röding's signature. On the other hand he cannot under-stand why he has to endure ridiculous official functions, put up with long meetings and argue with tedious union officials. Röding on the other hand is unable to keep to the unwritten but strict rules of village life. Those around the two accept what they see as their quirks but firmly refuse to change their routine. Only the children have clearer vision: from the very first day of the switch they insist their fathers have gone mad.

As in a Boccaccio novella neither of the two wives realizes they have different husbands. That is not really surprising since they have long since avoided sharing their beds with them. Margarete is delighted that her husband has stopped drinking, that his gout has gone, that he is much less rude to her. Now she would most like to get rid of Anton, the labourer, and throw herself into Röding's arms. He has to resort to all kinds of excuses if he wants to be left in peace. That makes Margarete more and more determined to win her supposed husband back.

Things are the other way round in Röding's house. Klamm makes hesitant but clear approaches to Daniela, who is not at all enamoured of them. Passion, she says, ill becomes a man of his age. Nor does she like the rural habits he has assumed and determinedly keeps her bedroom to herself; Klamm doesn't dare to insist on his conjugal rights. At the Press Ball, where his behaviour is 'outrageous', he causes a scandal. And in the newspaper offices the staff start secretly making fun of their boss. Klamm, who has by now become accustomed to his new role, is furious when he hears about it.

Things are coming to a head in Unklaich as well. The early rising, the hard physical labour and the boredom are as much of a problem to Röding as Margarete's advances, that are completely unwelcome to him. The labourer is jealous and finds Röding's attempts to create order on the farm ridiculous. He is no longer enjoying his 'holiday' from his real self and has soon had enough of the 'simple life' he used to dream about. He suddenly starts claiming he isn't Klamm at all but of course no one believes him now. The people in the village say he has delusions of grandeur and imagines he's a millionaire. Margarete sees his fantasies as an attempt to get rid of her. Philomela, Klamm's mother, is behind the visit of the village priest, who urges Röding to abandon his unchristian fantasies and to return to his wife.

Eventually Röding rings Daniela who, however, tells him icily that her husband is sitting beside her at the breakfast table and she will not tolerate being pestered with such stupid calls. After a second attempt she threatens to report the 'imposter' to the police. Röding realizes he will get nowhere with her. Secretly he even starts to doubt his memory. He curses his attempt to find a new life and his chauffeur who has left him stuck in Unklaich.

The newspaper is threatened with serious problems. It turns out that Schlicke can handle the day-to-day running of the business but is incapable of making major decisions. Klamm, for his part, operates with a combination of peasant cunning and honesty. He hasn't learnt to lie fluently, a defect that is bound to lead to the ruin of the small firm sooner or later. Things aren't going well at home either. The old lady despises him, the children think he's a fool and Daniela is recalcitrant. By now he's totally fed up with his life as a fine gentleman. In the course of an argument with his wife he finally tells her that he's not that ridiculous crook and moneybags Röding but a farmer from Unklaich called Klamm. At this not only the family but the people in the newspaper offices as well think he's certifiable. The old lady calls in a psychiatrist, Dr Maltzan, who examines him and diagnoses a typical 'manager psychosis'.

Klamm confides in Lucky, who continues to behave as if he thinks he's Röding. The chauffeur tells him the family intends to have him sent to a clinic. Klamm begs him to help him escape somewhere, no matter where. As the ambulance with the medical orderlies drives up, Lucky manages to help his master escape through the garden. Pursued by the ambulance siren, they manage to get to the airport and charter a small plane that Lucky flies himself.

Over a godforsaken stretch of land, far from the town, the engine goes on fire. Lucky, a triumphant smile of his face tells Klamm to jump at once. While Klamm is swinging under his parachute, the plane crashes, apparently with Lucky on board.

Röding, too, can think of no other way out than to head off into the unknown. The quarrel between Röding, Magareta and Philomena escalates. He gathers up what little possessions he has and leaves the farm, heading for the road.

When Klamm lands, he looks around and sees the chicken-coop of his own farm in the distance. Röding has reached the highway and is desperately trying to hitch a lift from one of the cars whizzing past. The sixth brakes and comes to a halt. At the wheel is Lucky, who doffs his cap, politely opens the door for his master and greets him without the least sign of surprise, as if nothing had happened. Röding gets in and the limousine goes off into the twilight.

Die Spanische Wand[4]

Spain, autumn 1962. When the Cold War is at its height, the United Nations' boycott of the Spanish dictator Franco is close to collapse. The Caudillo is haggling with the USA for a treaty that would secure strategically important bases on the peninsula for the West. In return he will receive economic aid that will enable him to modernize the run-down country.

Two German businessmen, who are to negotiate with Spanish partners on their firms' behalf, meet in a hotel in Madrid. Kornheim and Dr Klett are between 40 and 45 years old. Both can speak Spanish very well. Given the sluggish nature of the local bureaucracy, the decisions of the ministry and the banks are a long time coming. The two men are bored and seeking comfort at the hotel bar. Kornheim reveals that he is a member of the board of a large Düsseldorf company—they are planning to build an assembly plant in Aragon—while Dr Klett gives

---

4 Literally 'the Spanish wall' but actually means a 'folding screen'.

evasive answers to that kind of question. The two start discussing the Federal government's policy towards East Germany
and the threat of a war because of the conflict in Korea. Something about the way Klett talks leads Kornheim to suspect the
other is pursuing the interests of the GDR. Initially he denies
this, pointing out that there are no official relations between the
communist countries and Spain. That doesn't satisfy Kornheim;
he's convinced he's dealing with an emissary from East Berlin.
From a few hints he guesses that Klett fought on the Republican
side during the Spanish Civil War, probably even with the International Brigades. He tells Klett this to his face, and the latter
suspects that Kornheim is also familiar with the civil war from
personal experience. Kornheim, driven into a corner, is forced to
admit that he served with the Fifth Regiment, a Comintern organization. Late in the night the conversation at the bar concen-
trates on a particular section of the Aragon Front without it
becoming clear what kind of role either of the two played there.

First flashback. Following the *Rashomon*-principle, Klett's version
is shown first. An episode in a village that is being fought over.
The priest's sympathies are with the Republic, the landowner's
with the Falangists. Both are old and confused. As the front line
is constantly changing a tragi-comedy develops: now one of
them has to hide from the enemy who wants to kill him, now
the other. The two are played by the actors taking Klett's and
Kornheim's parts.

There follows Kornheim's version of the same events. While
the landowner secretly gave the Republicans valuable assistance,

the priest was a fool whom Franco's troops mistakenly murdered in cold blood.

Back to the meeting of the two Germans in Madrid. Kornheim is convinced that Klett's version cannot be correct, that he has something to hide. Since he has good contacts—he is invited out hunting by the Duke of Jungera and associates with Franco's senior officials—he makes enquiries among the Falangists. He learns that Klett was not, as he claims, in the International Brigades but had fought on Franco's side with the German Condor Legion, and not as a minor foot-soldier but as a feared fanatic. Kornheim confronts him with the results of his research and Klett has no choice but to confirm them. However, he assures him that his comrades in East Berlin knew about his past, claiming he had told them about it when he joined the Socialist Unity Party. They believed that his conversion to communism was genuine and he had been sent to Spain precisely because of his past: he knew the victors from personal experience which gave him an advantage in negotiations. A vehement argument develops between the two businessmen and they reproach each other for their behaviour in the past and the present.

Second flashback. A confrontation after the Battle of Teruel in February 1938. Kornheim's version of the events is as follows: while retreating he is captured by the Republicans and tortured by Klett.

Klett sees the events quite differently: Kornheim was spying for the communists behind the line, so he had no choice but to interrogate him.

During an encounter in Retiro Park the antagonists each indicate how they could put pressure on the other. If the East Germans should learn what Klett did in the past both his position and his life would be in danger. On the other hand, things could become difficult for Kornheim in his Düsseldorf company if they should learn that he had been a militant communist in the past. Each could ruin the other's career. They see the parallels between their situations and, during a night in which they get drunk, agree a truce.

In the course of all this they get closer to each other. They finally talk openly about their politically motivated crimes. Back then Klett coordinated the bombing of civilian targets in the Basque country and Kornheim, as an agent of the Comintern, was involved in the liquidation of the Trotskyites in Barcelona. Each explains to the other how their ideological turnaround came about. During the evening two German biographies mirror each other.

When the civil war was lost Kornheim managed to escape to Portugal. For a few years he continued to work for the Soviet Union as a result of his anti-fascist convictions but had contacts with both the German and the Allied sides. Broke and by then completely disillusioned in Lisbon after the end of the war he met Otto von Amerongen, an influential German businessman who recognized his talents as a manager and helped him to establish himself in German industry.

Disappointed with National Socialism, Klett joined the German army as an officer, was captured in Russia and joined the National Committee for a Free Germany. There he was converted to Marxism and decided to become involved in establishing the East German state.

A few weeks later Klett surprisingly invites his drinking companion to a farewell meal in the Horcher. Both are familiar with the Madrid restaurant—it was always the preferred meeting place for dubious deals and all kinds of agents. While Kornheim's negotiations have failed, Klett can report a success. In both cases it was a matter of armaments. The GDR wants to buy night-vision devices secretly for their border guards, but for the Düsseldorf concern it's too soon for the assembly plant they plan to build in Aragon: the Spanish lack foreign currency and the Germans political backing. Even though Klett has been successful, they both get drunkenly maudlin. 'Germans at one table,' they say, that's just a latrine rumour; here in Madrid you can only laugh at that idea. As for reunification, 'Nobody gives a damn about that.' They discover more and more similarities: both have been betrayed in the course of their lives, one by Stalin, the other by Hitler. Nothing much will remain of the Spain they know. Soon it will be a country like all the others where people go to sit on the beach, to play golf and enjoy their twilight years. By then the civil war, in which they both failed, will be merely a reminiscence, an occasion for remembrance and anniversary

celebrations. The fraternization of the two betrayed traitors ends
with them staggering through the deserted streets of Madrid,
babbling away to themselves.

The Three Wise Men from the Orient

You don't have to imagine the conferences of the TV-programme directors in Mainz and elsewhere, but if you do it leaves you feeling pretty depressed. Even in February it's all about December. As every year, the festive season is looming. What, for Christ's sake are we going to put on for Christmas and the New Year this time? The same stuff, year after year? Perhaps we should give these poor gentlemen a hand so that they can spare viewers a repeat of the tedious review of the year and the hoary Christmas tale of the nutcracker.

That doesn't have to happen, of course. The demand for our advice is doubtless limited, but that doesn't bother us. Let's just think up a little show. It's 1989. A few decades either way don't matter and the Three Kings will hardly be bothered if they never appear on our screens again.

CHARACTERS

The Three Wise Men: Caspar, Melchior and Balthazar are visitors from the Middle East. At first sight all viewers will identify them as 'oil sheikhs', for they will be wearing the *haik*, their typical white cloak, and the headdress that has by now become common in the streets of European cities; then sandals and, perhaps, daggers. Only at a second view will certain differences be noticed. Above all they will always be carrying presents in precious containers: gold in a bejewelled casket, frankincense and myrrh in a container like a monstrance or a bag decorated with pearls—designed after models from art, for example Dürer's *Adoration of the Magi* from the Uffizi. Fantasy divergences from the usual Beduin dress are a possibility, but should only be used sparingly so as not to make the Magi into figures of fun.

Following tradition, Caspar is the eldest, almost an old man; Melchior a man in the prime of life; Balthazar youthful and darkskinned, a Moor.

The Three Wise Men hardly speak at all. They respond to everything they experience during their journey with unwavering dignity and naivety and never lose their regal composure. A minimum of gestures and expressions: a faint smile, lowered eyelids, a shrug of the shoulders or an upward movement of the head indicating negation or rejection. Perhaps one of them will clap his hands softly at one point to call a servant. When they speak they will do so slowly, majestically, in an incomprehensible language—a dialect of Arabic, perhaps Chaldaean or Aramaic.

Understanding more or less always indirectly, through the Majordomo, who whispers in their ear what they need to know and then negotiates with the German Interpreter, so that it gives the impression of talebearing. You can never tell whether this kind of communication works; perhaps everything that happens is based on a series of misunderstandings; that is even to be assumed.

The Majordomo is a small, fat but surprisingly nimble man of around 40. He might make one think of Sancho Panza. He has peasant cunning and is unscrupulous. He wants to amuse himself and is looking to secure his own advantage in everything, he has a certain insolence and bows down to no one. He treats the Three Wise Men alone with absolute respect and deep devotion. He has a very long and complicated name but magnanimously tells Europeans, 'You can call me Malik, just Malik.'

His clothing is a motley collection of off-the-peg items, but gaudy and striking; he is wearing solid rings, a huge wristwatch and carries the latest mobile, etc. Dealing with technology is no problem for him—in contrast to the Three Wise Men who never pick up or use a machine or gadget.

The Interpreter, his German counterpart, is a shadowy, somewhat dubious figure. He tries to establish a pally relationship with Malik, which the Majordomo immediately susses out. The pair of them whisper to each other, give each other knowing looks. At the buffet the Interpreter stuffs delicacies and cigars in his pockets. He wears rimless spectacles and a rather shabby suit with a too-green tie.

The Head of Protocol, his employer, is an extremely punctilious civil-servant type, somewhat limited and apprehensive; he is constantly afraid of getting something wrong and therefore gets everything wrong. His problem is that he doesn't understand what the visit from the Orient is all about. He's not the only one but of course everything that goes wrong comes back to him. Grey tailored suit, regimental tie, so inconspicuous as to be conspicuous. Talks too much, tends to be a fusspot.

The Others are supporting roles or extras. It would be best to use amateur actors, as far as possible, and in general to see that the play be directed in a 'documentary style': real nurses, customs officers, officials and police.

The Mayor of Berlin only appears later on; if he is unwilling to take part himself, he will have to be replaced by a double who is as close to him as possible in stature, voice and bearing.

A Kuwait Airways plane: In the first class two of the three Wise Men are asleep. Balthazar alone is playing patience on the pulldown table.

Behind him Malik, the Majordomo, is reading an Arabic newspaper. A stewardess brings a trolly with food and drink, that Malik refuses. She goes back to her colleague in the pantry.

'They're refusing everything and demanding peppermint tea! Peppermint tea, I ask you! Has anyone here got some peppermint tea?'

The tea is made from a tube of Polo mints.

Malik whispers something in Balthazar's ear, who then looks out of the window. There's a huge star (cartoon) to be seen in the sky. Balthazar wakes the two old men. They all look out of the window, satisfied.

Things are getting hectic in the offices of the Berlin Senate. The Senate Administrator is calling the Senator in charge of domestic affairs, who is outraged that he should be woken by the ringing of the phone. The call is about an announcement that has just arrived from the overnight duty officer at the Foreign Office:

Top priority. The FO can announce the flying visit of three top-ranking guests from the Gulf States. More precise details of their diplomatic status are not yet available, enquiries are still being made of the embassy in Abu Dhabi; it is assumed they are emirs or heirs to the throne from Al Fujairah or Umm Al Quwain.

The Senate Administrator asks where the hell that is. The Head of Protocol has a servant bring an atlas. The FO emphasizes that vital economic interests of the Federal Republic are at stake. 'Suggest full formal programme including exports, mining, chemistry, information technology, etc., after consulting the Department of Trade and Industry, Chambers of Industry and Commerce if at all possible. Grand reception in the Senate indispensable to complete supporting cultural programme.' Unfortunately the Head of Section 3 has gone away for Christmas; nor have they been able to contact the relevant regional department. People are wondering whether the Mayor should not be woken. The visitors will probably be accompanied by a whole army of bodyguards and servants, possibly even a complete harem! Interpreters are being called but because it's the holiday period only one is available; he is being engaged immediately.

When is the plane actually due to land? And which national anthem is to be played at the airport, given that they don't know which of the Emirates their visitors actually come from. They have no recording of the anthem of the United Arab Emirates, moreover the police band couldn't play it. Do they have a national anthem at all, anyway? Eventually a secretary suggests they send the Schöneberg Boys' Choir to the airport. General sighs of relief: that's the solution.

It's snowing at Tegel Airport. The terminal is a riot of Christmas decorations. The reception committee is waiting. Security is everywhere, some in uniform with machine pistols and crackling walkie-talkies, some in trench coats. A red carpet is rolled out. The first of the paparazzi appear. The Head of Protocol is discussing with the Interpreter which form of greeting is appropriate. Handshake? Embrace and kisses on the cheeks? Or simply stand there, bow then wait and see what happens? Are bouquets usual in Arabia? If they are, who should present them? How should one behave if there are ladies in the entourage? The

Interpreter, who puts on a show of being an expert, is horrified. Shake hands? For God's sake no! These people are sensitive.

Eventually the plane lands. The boys' choir is at the ready. The Three Wise Men cautiously hold out their hands to check the exotic snow, smell it and taste it. Not a word of the greeting at the gangway can be understood. The attempt at a kiss on the cheeks fails because the Head of Protocol gets the wrong person, namely Malik, who pushes to the front. The Choirmaster has his hands raised. We can see the choirboys' wide-open mouths but hear nothing until the jets have been switched off. The Choirmaster starts again:

> Standing alone in the darkling night
> in my yearning heart your stars shine bright;
> far ahead my wishes have flown,
> longing to be with you alone,
> waiting for me, in my distant home.
> Home! Your starry display
> still shines for me
> in this land far away.
> Their message I gladly see
> as the tender words of love.
> The fair hour of morning,
> the sky all ablaze
> with stars in the dawning—
> A promise of happier days.

(Text by Erik Knauf. Music by Werner Bochman, 1941, from the film *Quax der Bruchpilot*.)

The style of the boys' choir is, as is usual in Advent recordings on German TV, to be scrupulously respected: completely serious delivery, as if they were singing a Christmas carol. Only the inter-cut shots show the bustle of the airport, Malik picking his nose, the Head of Protocol nervously looking at his watch and the Three Wise Men listening politely, though astonished and baf-fled.

The Three Wise Men have withdrawn to their suite in their lodg-ings. In the sitting room Malik is seeing to their luggage. Carpets are unrolled, hookahs set up, daggers hung from the walls. The room takes on the look of a tent.

It proves impossible to shake off the German Interpreter. He's particularly interested in the caskets and vessels with the presents. May I? He sniffs the frankincense and myrrh to see whether its hashish. He tries to do a deal with Malik and rum-mages through his briefcase, taking out all sorts of things he offers: mobile, CD player, porn magazine. Malik shows no interest. Out of a bundle he pulls half a lamb, firewood, a poker, a copper pan, a large tin sheet and a trestle. He turns out his pockets looking for matches. The Interpreter immediately pro-duces his lighter. Malik takes it, paying for it with a gold coin out of his pocket. Then he lights the fire. It smokes. Outside the Interpreter is whispering to the security officer. The alarm is given. Firemen and reporters with cameras appear in the corri-dor. The firemen, who have brought axes, break open the door. Malik is dancing around his little fire. The Three Wise Men in their beds don't notice anything. They sleep on.

They are given the tour of the city in the morning. It is snowing. The Three Wise Men are in a stretch limousine, accompanied by Malik, an official from the Protocol Section, the Interpreter and a Guide who rattles off his spiel in English. What can he heard is a recording of a normal bus journey. The translator repeats what the Guide says in Arabic. The Three Wise Men show no reaction. They simply smile and give each other meaningful looks.

All that can be seen of the Reichstag is some builder's fence with graffiti; by the Gedächtniskirche above all the homeless, souvenir shops and hot-dog stands. They are driven to one of the few remnants of the Berlin Wall; the Three Wise Men have no idea what it's all about and refuse to get out of the car. The protocol official tries to explain. Via the Interpreter Malik announces the guests' response, 'Very excellent! Beautiful city.'

In the zoo they're taken to see the camels, that make a sad impression. On the Kurfürstendamm beggars with self-made signs; alms are immediately distributed to them. There's not much call for frankincense and myrrh. One or two trippers try to stuff the weed in their pipes. Malik distributes gold coins out of the casket, which causes a riot. The car drives on but keeps getting stuck in traffic jams and held back by snow ploughs and other vehicles clearing the streets.

As they drive on Malik discovers a few skateboarders and insists on trying out this unknown sport; he's also interested in jugglers and people selling toys such as fluorescent yoyos or Mutzi the Magic Worm. The Three Wise Men look on patiently while the man from Protocol is getting nervous and urges them to continue.

The Europa Centre with the Mercedes star (large). Malik feels at home in Kreuzberg.[5] He sniffs at a falafel stall and whispers with the Three Wise Men. The guests express the wish to go over to it in order finally to eat a familiar dish.

Last stop on the tour of the city: the mosque in Wilmersdorf. The Three Wise Men seem to have no desire to visit it. Inside it looks dull and bare. As they hurry out they see, poised outside in front of the building, the inevitable boys' choir, shivering in the snowstorm. They sing:

When there are grey skies,
I don't mind grey skies
You make them blue,
Sonny Boy.
Friends may forsake me.
Let them all forsake me,
Sonny Boy

(*Sonny Boy*, 1929. Text and music by Bud de Sylva, Lew Brown, Ray Andersen, Al Jonson.)

The lecture theatre in the House of World Cultures is far too big for the sparse audience. Present are officials of the Senate, Orientalists, students, the occasional veiled lady, plus a German

---

5 Earlier known to be one of the poorest areas of the city, a neighbourhood of immigrants, predominantly of Turkish origin— over the years, Kreuzberg has evolved into a popular centre of the counterculture.

convert in Islamic dress. On the platform are an expert on the Middle East, representatives of the Senate, a professor of Religious Studies, a politician from the Green Party.

The Senate official is so cautious in the way he talks about the Three Wise Men that no one has any idea who they actually are. Applause and catcalls in the hall. The professor has to be interrupted because he's threatening to deliver an extensive lecture on his research into the origins of Oriental religions in antiquity. The expert on the Middle East sees the origin of the region's problems in the lack of water. The Green politician brings up the justified demands of the Palestinians, supported by students in the audience holding up placards. There are shouts condemning the manipulations of the oil conglomerates.

The young blond convert in the front row grabs the microphone and recounts how he came to the West from Grimma in the GDR, saw the futility of consumerism and read the Koran. At the end he introduces himself: he is now called Abdullah Salam Al Hakim. All of this in the Saxon accent of East Germany. Protests and mocking laughter from the left-wing group. A shot of the podium: the Three Wise Men have fallen asleep.

When the drive continues they park outside one of the typical Berlin educational refineries, a huge concrete block with pipes painted red, yellow and blue on the roof. In the corridors daubed with many colours, the cries of children can already be heard. The security officers see to security. There is a different kind of chaos going on in every room: adolescents who have tied their female teacher to the map-stand; kids in the first year throwing books, satchels, and bits of school dinner at each other. Only the fourth door opened turns out to be the right one. Everything has been prepared there: an oasis of peace: a kindergarten teacher with delightfully dressed, well-mannered four- to five-year-olds, who jump to their feet as soon as the visitors enter and intone 'Good morning, dear visitors from the Orient.' The girls curtsey, the boys bow. A decorated Christmas tree is shown. The children dance around it and sing in falsetto tones:

We three kings of oil and tar
tried to smoke a smelly cigar.
It was loaded, it exploded,
now we're all orbiting Mars.

The teacher looks on proudly. For the first time the Three Wise Men, completely baffled, turn tail and flee.

For the following scene the best thing would be to use archive film of a genuine state reception. Even better would be to sneak the Three Wise Men, Malik, the Head of Protocol and the Interpreter into a genuine Senate reception; then the curious stares and comments of the invited guests at the exotic strangers could be recorded on the spot. Alexander Kluge's camera-work could be used as a model.

The reception is intercut with shots behind the scenes: the bodyguards refusing to hand in their weapons at the cloakroom, the kitchen, the severely disabled janitor, etc. What is shown are the typical events and non-events of that kind of reception: the permanent good-humoured expression on the Mayor's face, the starlets and their managers, businessmen discussing tax-efficient operations, etc. As always, the buffet is descended upon and cleared in a matter of minutes, not least by Malik and the Interpreter. A few scraps from the speeches of welcome off-camera, none of the speakers is seen: 'Bearing in mind the traditional friendship between our countries . . .'—'. . . it gives me quite particular pleasure . . .'—'. . . in the hope of even closer collaboration in the political, economic and cultural field . . .' The Three Wise Men are offered champagne, which they refuse with thanks and a weary raising of their eyelids. A man from the Chamber of Industry and Commerce offers a present and a token of respect from the economic partners in Berlin. It is almost the height of a man and is unveiled by two women: a huge china camel from the Royal Porcelain Factory in Berlin (plaster model). At first the Three Wise Men don't realize the camel is for them but graciously accept it after Malik has explained. For the first and only time they make a speech, each with one sentence in Aramaic which Malik, this time absolutely serious, translates into perfect German.

Caspar. 'Take the treasure of wisdom by which thou wilt rule in justice over thy people; for the honour of a king is as gold.'

Melchior. 'Take the frankincense of humility and quiet gentleness; by these wilt thou raise up those in need.'

Balthazar. 'Take the myrrh of penitence by which thou wilt curb the enticing lures of thy greed.'

The gentlemen from the Chamber of Commerce are dismayed. The Head of Protocol tries to rescue the situation by getting the band to play *Berliner Luft*. Then he turns and says to Malik in confidential tones, 'And now, my dear Herr Malik, we have something very special for Their Excellencies. For our city also has its enjoyable side. All work and no play makes Jack a dull boy, eh? *Joie de vivre* is in the air in Berlin. Therefore to complete their day our guests will see how Berlin enjoys itself.'

Tour buses outside a night club. '*See Berlin by Night*'. The security officers form a cordon. Entry of the Three Wise Men with their entourage. Catcalls and ironic cheers from the regulars. The end of one of the ordinary turns is seen, the dancers dressed in nothing but a few stars covered in glitter. Then, after the usual kind of announcement, a belly dancer appears on stage. Pseudo-oriental music. After her performance the belly dancer approaches the guests of honour. Although described as 'Fatima with the miracle belly from the forbidden palaces of North Yemen' she speaks pure Cologne German. Malik gets Fatima to sit at his table, but only when she's on his lap and her stage voice reverts to its normal bass does he realize that Fatima is a man. When the belly dancer shows too much interest in their caskets, the Three Wise Men get up and leave the night club.

The boys' choir has already appeared on the snowy pavement outside. Among their audience are rent boys, pimps, prostitutes and drunks. They sing:

Just look at those stars,
up there in the sky—
and now I must leave you
though I can't say why.
A day like today's
will for ever remain
locked in my heart
till we two meet again.

(German: *So ein Tag*, 1954. Lyrics by Walther Rothenburg. Music by Lotar Olias.)

The next morning there is a visit to the research laboratory of a pharmaceutical firm. The Three Wise Men, accompanied by the Head of Protocol and an official of the Senate economic committee. The only one who is interested in the technology is Malik who, as always, fools around, flirts with the female lab assistants and creates disorder. Conference room with tubular-steel chairs and a precisely arranged table: in front of each participant the same array of bottles, glasses, ball-points, brochures and notepads. The chairman thanks the visitors from one of the most important regions of the world economy, talks about the potential for development, petrodollars, venture capital, credit facilities and Federal guarantees. Possibly leading to a power-point presentation.

We only hear scraps of all this for it keeps being intercut with shots of men in the toilet. We hear initially cautious then less and less restrained complaints about the Three Wise Men's lack of interest: Do you know anything about this Emirate?—Do they have any oil at all?—They're not really listening anyway!—And I specially skipped a meeting in Dortmund.—We're barking up the wrong tree here.—We're obviously talking to the wrong people. They've no idea. Most of the men speak standard German in the conference room but Berlin dialect in the toilet.

Finally they corner the Senate official: What were you thinking of? Who are these people anyway?—We were advised of their arrival by the Foreign Office.—So what? Have you checked what it's all about?—They've no intention of placing orders.—Bribes won't help either, on the contrary they were even offering me gold and some herbs.—Perhaps they're not the genuine article.—Conmen, perhaps, who're taking us for a ride. The Head of Protocol enters the toilet and now he's the scapegoat. When Malik arrives as well, he tells them that Their Excellencies have had enough of Berlin and want to leave. The Head of Protocol protests. He wants to stick to his programme: just one more visit to go.

A resolute Matron has taken up position outside the entrance to a hospital maternity ward, if possible a Catholic nun with a wimple. It's not visiting time, she says. The Head of Protocol exercises his authority. In the ward, behind glass, the Three Wise Men are shown a row of cots with newborn babies in them. They try to give the children presents but that is simply going too far for the Matron. Any objects that haven't been disinfected are out of the question, she insists. Doctor intervenes. Wouldn't the gentlemen like to take a seat in the nurses' common room, there's coffee on the go there. They are taken into a rather dreary place with waiting-room chairs, children's drawings and posters explaining everything that is forbidden there.

The boys' choir has taken up position in front of a glass door, behind which more infants can be seen. As a mother with a happy smile on her face and a child in her arms is led in, the choir starts to sing a song:

Sweetie, my little sweetie-pie
Sweetie, the apple of my eye
Sweetie, my darling sweetie,
I'm asking you, oh love me, do.
Sweetie, you look just divine,
Sweetie, oh were you mine!
Sweetie, my darling sweetie,
Be so fine, give me the sign
That you'll be mine.

(German: *Püppchen*, 1929. Words by Alfred Schönfeld. Music by Jean Gilbert.)

After that the camera will discover a manger in one corner of the room, set up with the stall, the baby Jesus, Mary and Joseph, angels, the ox and the ass, illuminated by a big star. It shows the adoration of the Magi. For the first time the Three Wise Men respond with lively, joyful interest. Now the truth begins to dawn on the Head of Protocol. He hurries into the corridor and takes out his mobile. 'The Foreign Minister's office. Very, very urgent.

It's about the three Arab visitors.'—'No, please listen to me first. —I am Head of Protocol for the Senate, Minister, Lehmann's my name. No, we don't know each other, I'm new here, I used to be manager of the Cleansing Department. It's about the state visit.—We don't exactly know that ourselves, but the Foreign Office asked us for assistance, because of the holidays.—Three gentlemen from the Emirates.—We thought that too at first, but they've been behaving in a very strange way, I was getting quite desperate. Politics, no interest; industry none, nightlife, nothing. The Senate reception was a catastrophe, so we tried a maternity home. Human interest, you understand . . . No, please don't hang up, that's wasn't a joke. The boys' choir has just sung *Sweetie*—What, you don't know *Sweetie*? Doesn't matter. Anyway, I had a look at the manger and who did I see there? Our visitors! To the life! The same build, the same clothes, the same get-up and holding the same caskets and presents.—God only knows what's in them.—So the Middle East Section has to help us out.—Exactly, Minister, it's more something for the Catholic side, I've already tried but I couldn't get through to the Archbishop. The Senate Manager begs you to help, it's a matter of urgency.— I'm also thinking of the press. The plane leaves in two hours.— Please, just a few appropriate words of farewell—No? Or your junior minister as a substitute?—Not him either?

The Head of Protocol collapses in the corridor.

It's stopped snowing, instead it's raining heavily. The Three Wise Men are waiting in the departure lounge with their entourage.

Their plane can be seen on the runway. This time it's a private plane with Arabic markings. A pilot in a burnous salutes. The Head of Protocol, agitated, keeps consulting his watch.

A car with a blue light drives up outside. The Archbishop, in full regalia, gets out, hurries into the building and knocks on the glass wall behind which the Three Wise Men are sitting. The customs officials refuse to let the cleric pass through. Dialogue in mime with the Three Wise Men who want to hand their gifts over to the Archbishop. The priest thanks them, puts his hands either side of his mouth and shouts something incomprehensible to them and returns the blessing.

The Three Wise Men on the runway. The boys' choir is already waiting in front of the plane with their song:

Now the sound of war
rings out on Turkey's shore,
Europe's arming without cease.
Our hearts are gripped with fear,
our lips beg, loud and clear:
Will no one bring us peace?
Hear our plea we beg you all,
Don't turn a deaf ear to our call.
Fly away, O little dove,
beyond the dark'ning clouds above,
bring from the stars unfurled
peace unto the world.

(*Flieg, du kleine Rumplertaube*, 1912. Words by Alfred Schönfeld. Music by Jean Gilbert.) During their performance the plane taxies and then takes off.

In the cabin the Three Kings, relieved, with happy smiles on their faces, are smoking a hookah. Malik is playing with his acquisitions: Play Station, telecamera, film cassettes.

In the departure lounge the Head of Protocol wipes the sweat from his brow.

The boys' choir's third verse is relayed over the loudspeakers:
Rising in the sky,
Soaring up on high
Is a very modern dove.
As in Noah's days,
It sets our hearts ablaze
With its song of love.
Fly away, O little dove,
beyond the dark'ning clouds above,
bring from the stars unfurled
peace unto the world.

While the boys are finishing their song, the Archbishop watches the plane fly off. In the sky the star of Bethlehem is huge.

Our last sight of the Three Wise Men is of them going across the desert on foot with their entourage, getting smaller and smaller until they disappear.

Fraternal Strife

I have always been surprised that, apart from Wolfgang Koeppen, whose novel *Das Treibhaus* (*The Hothouse*) appeared as early as 1953, no writer has dealt with the problem of the rearmament of the Federal Republic. Least of all was the German film industry's interest in the subject. They preferred to make films about happy country life such as *Grün ist die Heide* (1951), *Der Förster vom Silberwald* (1954) and *Die Christel von der Post* (1956). Nor could the 'New German Film' make much of the pacifist feelings in German society and the conflicts resulting from them. And that despite there being some very useful source material available in the 1980s at the latest, when the so-called Peace Movement was at its height. It was therefore not necessary to go to the archives to realize that it was a conflict that played a decisive role in the history of the two German republics. A few publicly available publications are enough to provide a survey of the question:

Aspekte der deutschen Wiederbewaffnung bis 1955 [Aspects of German Rearmament up to 1955] with contributions from H. Buchheim and others (1975);

Gerhard Wettig, *Entmilitarisierung und Wiederbewaffnung in Deutschland 1943–1955* [Demilitarization and Rearmament in Germany 1943–1955] (1967);

Fritz Kopp, *Chronik der Wiederbewaffnung in Deutschland* [Chronicle of Rearmament in Germany] (1958);

and a later publication, for example:

Stefan Stosch, *Die Adenauer-Legion, Geheimauftrag Wiederbewaffnung* [The Adenauer Legion, a Secret Mission to Rearm] (1994).

The notes I made back then will contain nothing new for contemporary historians but everyone else seems to have forgotten the fantastic game played out behind the scenes:

A Brief Chronicle

1945

General Reinhard Gehlen, head of the 'Foreign Armies East' section in the Army general staff, puts the material of his secret service at the disposal of the American occupying force.

1947

The Cold War is looming. Given the threat of the Soviet Union the American government is considering rearming West Germany.

In early August, Walter Ulbricht tells the members of the Central Secretariat of the Socialist Unity Party that in the last few months the Soviet Military Administration had started to make organizational preparations for setting up a 'powerful centralized police force.'

At the end of 1947, Hans Speidel, former general, has talks with the future federal minister Hermann-Eberhard

Wildermuth in Tübingen and Freudenstadt about Germany's security requirements.

1948

At the meeting of the heads of the German federal states in Munich 1947, Hans Ehard of the CDU had said to his permanent secretary, 'Just imagine . . . they want us to rearm.' In July 1948, the Soviet military administration in East Berlin decrees the setting-up of armed units stationed in barracks that are to become the nucleus of the National People's Army. By the end of 1948 they have 7,500 men; by the end of 1950, they have 70,000.

At the request of Carlo Schmidt, Hans Speidel prepares a memorandum on German rearmament. In his analysis, Speidel concludes that neutrality was not an option, that the Western allies had to guarantee the security of West Germany and set up a West European defence community. On 19 July, he presents these results to Carlo Schmidt, Theodor Heuss, Theodor Eschenburg and other selected politicians and journalists. In the middle of November, Speidel submits two further memoranda to Konrad Adenauer in which he concludes that they had to be prepared in order to make a contribution to their own defence, including tank corps if necessary. These units would be integrated into a multinational West European army. A prerequisite was the formation of self-contained German units under German command and German officers working in the joint staffs on an equal footing with the others.

The first articles discussing Speidel's ideas begin to appear, without naming him, in the German press. While Russian forces are blockading West Berlin, Rudolf Augstein reviews in *Spiegel* the advantages and risks of a German 'volunteer army'. Speidel, who was born in 1897 in Metzingen, had been a regular officer during the First World War and on the German general staff from 1939 to 1944, eventually under Rommel. After 20 July 1944, the attempted assassination of Hitler, he was arrested as a confidant of General Beck. Later he served as Adenauer's military adviser and between 1957 and 1963 he was commander-in-chief of the NATO land forces in Central Europe.

1949

In March, Adenauer tells a United Press journalist that it was 'one of the major tasks of a West German government' to bring about full membership of NATO, which at the time had not yet been set up; it was hardly conceivable without West German troops. Speidel is demanding complete equality, the termination of the state of war, German divisions under German command, equipped with modern weapons, including tanks and an operational air force. These ideas are vehemently rejected at home and abroad. 'No more war!' The question of rearmament should not be considered seriously at all, is what is said in the German and French press.

NATO is founded in April and a few weeks later the German constitution is promulgated; it makes no provision for armed forces. In the Occupation Statute, that comes into power in

September, the Western Allies reserve to themselves the responsibility for 'disarmament and demilitarization'. In October the GDR is founded. At Harvard, General Clay argues in favour of rearming West Germany. There are no protests to be heard against that plan in America. On the other hand the British government states that they have no intention of agreeing to the formation of West German armed forces. France as well is saying that there is 'absolutely no question' of re-establishing German military power. In December, Adenauer in an interview with the *Cleveland Plain Dealer* suggests ('if necessary') the formation of a West European army with West German contingents; the next day he tells the German Press Agency that he wants to 'make it clear once and for all' that he is 'against the rearmament of the Federal Republic of Germany as a matter of principle and therefore against the establishment of a Germany army.'

1950

In May the 'Schwerin Office', the forerunner of the Blank Department, is set up and housed in the attic of Schaumburg Palace in Bonn under the code name of 'Agency for Homeland Service'. Three of its subsidiary offices are called 'Archive for Contemporary Research', 'Godesberg Assessment Office' (to check future personnel) and 'Committee of Experts'. Its main object is called 'internal security'. Ex-General Gerhard Count Schwerin recalls, 'Before I took over this department in the Federal Chancellor's Office, I set two conditions. In the first place my appointment had to be approved by the Americans and the French, as well as by the English, who had of course proposed me. The Americans gave their approval, if somewhat unenthusiastically, for they already had Gehlen, of course. The French weren't asked, they were left out but then they agreed.'

Representatives of the British and American secret services are now regular visitors to the Schwerin Office. When the crisis breaks out in Korea Adenauer, as Count Schwerin reports, receives a massive demand from General Hays, the military adviser to the American High Commissioner: The Third World War is imminent; we must start setting up German defence forces at once . . . Naturally the negotiations were top secret . . . Then we were . . . taken by the backstairs and through the kitchen into General Hays' rooms . . . The English and the French were not actively involved in this. It was a purely American affair, a purely American demand. The Federal Chancellor had to be extremely cautious in dealing with this matter for at that time any such activity was strictly forbidden and liable to punishment with a prison sentence. If anyone hostile to the Chancellor had been able to prove what went on with General Hays and what happened in my Office, we would perhaps have met each other again in prison.

'The deputies came to the Bundestag, threatening that what Adenauer was doing was illegal and went far beyond what they wanted, for they didn't want a contribution to defence. This "leave-me-out mood" predominated in the cabinet as well. At the conference of foreign ministers after the acute stage of the Korea crisis had come to an end, France, but then Britain as well, severely reproached the Americans, which forced them to call off the Germans. That meant that the Chancellor had been compromised and a sacrifice had to be found. That is presumably one of the reasons why I had to leave the Office.'

In August, Vice Chancellor Franz Blücher lets the cat out of the bag: he talks about secret weapons stores, mobilization plans and the imminent establishment of a West German army. A denial is issued immediately. Adenauer once more declares that he is against rearmament. Schumacher says that even discussing the matter is absurd. Fritz Reuter says he is 'strictly against rearmament', etc., etc.

At the same time at the request of Hermann-Eberhard Wildermuth (Housing Minister), Speidel, Heusinger and Foertsch, compile a memorandum that is presented to Adenauer: 'Thoughts on the external security of the Federal Republic of Germany.' Adenauer wants a guarantee from the Western powers that no German contribution of troops will be allowed without the right to have a say in political matters. Thereupon the Federal government declares itself for the first time as officially in favour of 'defence troops' for the Federal Republic.

Count Schwerin goes on: 'Adenauer had many obstacles to overcome in parliament. I have to say that all the actions he undertook were at that time illegal and subject to severe penalties. All negotiations had to be held in secret . . . We said that if that was the case, then our Office is too small and not authorized to make binding decisions on such matters. First of all, we must have a political representative in parliament for these things, in other words a minister of defence . . . They simply couldn't find one, for no one was willing to assume that responsibility. Eventually Adenauer found the unfortunate Theodor Blank for the task . . . What we needed now was a larger expert committee . . . That was how the Himmerod Conference came about, that was set up from my Office . . . Now that really did have to be kept secret; however since in those days nothing could be kept secret in Bonn, we were faced with a really big problem. Herr Blank had no idea what to do either, so we went to the old man and asked him. He just gave a cunning smile and said, "That's no problem, my friend, the Abbot of Himmerod Abbey will do it." '

In October, ten former generals and two admirals of the Wehrmacht meet there in strictest secrecy. The result is the 'Himmerod Memorandum': 'The act of procreation of the Bundeswehr (the German Army), the high point being Herr Heusinger's assessment of the situation . . . The operational system he presented was based on intelligence gathered by the "Gehlen Organization" . . . The problem of the "restoration of the honour of German soldiers" and the solution to the so-called "question of war criminals" . . . started in Himmerod.' First of all, the imprisoned generals had to be released, then 'the suspicions would melt away during a get-together with good wine, Abbey wine, for many the first since the war' (Adolf Count Kielmansegg).

'The Himmerod Memorandum . . . is the product of what the law in operation at the time called a conspiracy . . . What the Chancellor did then was in violation of the law of occupation that was valid at the time, in violation of international law. It makes a significant difference that, with Adenauer's knowledge, a group of people specially selected by Count Schwerin met under cloak-and-dagger conditions in an abbey, and that he should take cognizance of the result of their deliberations by adding them to official files. There is an anecdote that describes the atmosphere at the time. At the end of October 1950, a secretary in the attic of Schaumburg Palace told us that, shortly before or after Theodor Blank took office, an American in uniform delivered a heavy wooden box. The contents of the box—20 to 30 pistols with ammunition. A present for the Federal Chancellor's office. Now you must remember—at the time possession of firearms was still against the law for Germans, thus a political matter for the Chancellor's office. "I've no idea what happened to the guns . . . You will not be surprised that the staff of the Schwerin Office and Blank Department were unusually cautious. If the political climate should change signatures and initials could easily be interpreted as a conspiracy . . ."'(Bussche-Streithorst).

The opposition to rearmament is forming both inside and outside parliament. Minister of the Interior Gustav Heinemann protests against rearmament and is dismissed. The 'Count Me Out' campaign takes to the streets.

A so-called Blank Department is set up officially. Blank is appointed the 'Chancellor's commissioner for questions arising from the increase in allied forces.' As Kielmansegg reports, the assignment for Herr Blank was never put in writing. Heusinger and Speidel were asked whether they would be prepared 'to take part in this conspiracy with the Allies on the Petersberg, the seat of the Allied Control Commission . . . On Herr Blank's instructions I wrote those letters in code and on paper with my own private letter heading.'

1951

In January the three High Commissioners negotiate with representatives of the federal government together with Blank, Generals Heusinger and Speidel and a representative of the Foreign Office. The secretary was Colonel Count Kielmansegg: 'In individual discussions I have the impression that we find things more difficult with representatives of the CDU/CSU than with representatives of the SPD.'

1952

In February the Bundestag approves, against the votes of the opposition, a German contribution to defence.

1954

A change to the Basic Law allows the formation of the Bundeswehr.

1955

The Federal Republic joins NATO. The Warsaw Pact is set up. The government takes over the secret service that Gehlen has built up: the 'Gehlen Organization' that in 1956 is renamed the

'Federal Intelligence Service' and made directly responsible to the chancellor.

1956

The first Bundeswehr units go into operation. National service is introduced. The GDR National People's army is set up. Franz Josef Strauss is made defence minister.

INSTEAD OF AN OUTLINE

On the basis of this, admittedly minimal, information I one day worked out the storyline for a film that was roughly as follows below. I imagined the two main characters as brothers from the area around Siegen in North Rhine Westphalia, roughly in the middle of West Germany:

The older one, Bernhard, born 1904, has studied mechanical engineering. In 1935 he marries Marianne, a banker's daughter from a strict Catholic family; his only daughter, Gabriele, is born in 1936. In 1938 he takes over his father's firm, a steel and armaments company, and is deferred from military service. From 1943 onwards production is also carried on in the Protectorate of Bohemia and Moravia, using forced labour. The firm is flourishing. Bernhard is given the honorary rank of SS Führer but at the same time he is in contact with Thyssen and other industrialists who are already wondering how they will be able to secure their factories' survival after the war has been lost. Bernhard manages to save important senior staff and machines for the new beginning. His firm is

involved in the reconstruction of the ruined country from the outset because Bernhard immediately sees to it that he has good
relations with the British military government. He gets a divorce
in 1945 because he has started a relationship with his secretary.
At the end of 1947 he hears rumours of the rearmament of
Germany. At once he realizes what opportunities the Cold War
offers his firm and prepares for future armaments orders. In
1949 he separates from his lover and marries his first wife
Marianne again.

His younger brother, Reinhold, is born in 1912. At first he
studies theology, with the intention of becoming a priest, until
he meets his future wife in 1927 when he switches to law and
becomes a respected provincial lawyer. He had renounced his
inheritance while he was still in the seminary; for religious reasons he keeps himself at a distance from the Nazis, occasionally
acts as defence lawyer in political trials. He is called up in 1940,
initially as a military administrator, later he is sent to the front in
Russia and witnesses mass executions. He establishes relationships with officers who oppose the Nazis, is seriously wounded
in 1944 and returns home immediately after the end of the war.
In the meantime his wife has been killed in an air raid; the family
house is in ruins. At first he stays with his brother and establishes friendly relations with his wife. In 1947 he is one of the
founders of the CDU in Siegen (the Ahlen Programme), hands
over his chambers to a friend and is elected to the Bundestag
during the first elections.

The plot rests on the conflict between the two brothers that has its roots in their private life but comes to the surface on the political level. In Bonn Reinhard too hears rumours of the secret negotiations between Adenauer and the Allies' emissaries about the rearmament of Germany, with the involvement of men such as Gehlen and Globke, who have been severely compromised by their past. He is horrified. It is in blatant contradiction to the public protestations of his Party leaders and to his Christian convictions. He pursues the matter and discovers that his brother is one of those involved because he is a possible supplier of armaments and has good connections going back to the times of the Wehrmacht. He secretly searches through Bernhard's papers for proof, but Bernhard's secretary and lover detects Reinhard's clumsy researches. It comes to an open quarrel between the brothers. Bernhard warns him against going public with what he has found. To do that would endanger his life.

In the meantime Adenauer is recruiting less compromised officers from the Wehrmacht, a milieu in which Bernhard has a network from the war years. He meets his old comrades who keep him informed about the secret negotiations and the pressure from the Americans.

Reinhold confronts a leading member of the CDU with the results of his research. All he gets is denials. He discusses the matter with Bernhard's divorced wife, Marianne. That leads to a very Catholic love story in the manner of Heinrich Böll. She advises him not to go public without clear proof. Reinhold also makes contact with his niece Gabriele. He hesitates because he still hopes he is wrong. When, in December 1949, Adenauer finally admits what his intentions are, Reinhold realizes that rearmament has long since been decided on. He plans to lead the protest movement ('Count me out'). The Party drops him. Bernhard's wife goes back to her husband. Reinhold commits suicide. At the funeral Bernhard expresses doubts to his wife and a friend about whether his brother actually killed himself but does not pursue his suspicion himself. Gabriele is outraged, leaves her father's house and joins a left-wing fringe group.

The final shot shows the first parade of the Bundeswehr, with 1,500 men, in the presence of Adenauer; Bernhard and his wife can be seen on the rostrum.

The story is not without its ambiguities. It turns out that Reinhold definitely profited from the family fortune. In 1933 he was enthusiastic about Hitler. After his argument with his brother and as a member of parliament, but without his Party's knowledge, he received emissaries from the Soviet Zone, in the hope of getting information from the East and negotiated with them. In his relationship with Bernhard's wife Marianne he appears as inhibited and indecisive. All in all he is the good man who does not necessarily appeal to the audience.

Bernard, on the other hand, has charm aplenty; he's intelligent, generous and liked by women. He has a perspicacity his brother lacks. In political terms he turns out to be right. Bernhard, the villain, is at the same time the more attractive character.

Despite her strict Catholic upbringing Bernhard's wife, Marianne, is a sensuous woman, eager for life, who falls in love with Reinhold, in order to get her own back on Bernhard; they have an affair which she quickly finds disappointing. She can't understand her daughter's rebellion, she has no interest in politics. Even though she doesn't love Bernhard any longer, like him she wants to end up on the winning side.

This film project never got very far and, for understandable reasons, got stuck in my drawer; I have only brought it in here as evidence of the obliviousness to history of our little republic that by now is defending itself in the Hindu Kush.

The Smell of Art

THEMES

art theft; ambition; betrayal of love and eventual justice

SETTING

tax investigation, money laundering, the art trade on
a grand scale.

CHARACTERS

Julian Selk, 32, German tax investigator with good career
prospects, bachelor, dissatisfied with his bureaucratic job;

Blanka von Vezy, 26, art historian from an obscure background,
claims to be from Hungary, specialist in old masters;

Rudolf Braunschweig, 60, German businessman and art collector;

Jumeau, a representative of the Hirschfeld firm in 1940s occupied Paris, a collaborator;

David Hirschfeld, 65, billionaire, heir to and head of a dynasty
of art dealers with branches in New York, Paris and Zurich;

Amos Hirschfeld, 36, his son;

Officials of the German and the US tax authorities; a rich art collector; front men; French descendants of Holocaust victims.

GENRE

Formally the story should be constructed like a classic thriller,
though without the usual unambiguous morality. However,
this model should be repeatedly interrupted by quasi-documen-
tary interpolations. For example interviews with an expert in old
painting, an official from Interpol, a curator or art dealer, or shots
from a large-scale auction can be slotted in.

PLOT

Selk, a born sleuth, but with no background in or knowledge of
art, is bored in the office, even though he has scored some
striking successes. He meets Blanka, apparently by chance, and
starts an affair with her. She seduces him in a bare, temporary
apartment with wrapped-up pictures stacked against the walls.
Blanka goes with him to the museum and tries, initially in vain,
to get him interested in the great masters of painting.

In the office Selk is dealing with a money-laundering case.
He is investigating the business of Rudolf Braunschweig, a rich
import-export merchant from the provinces who is suspected of
tax evasion. He owns a large collection of art. The department

comes to an agreement with Braunschweig, is happy with a large payment of arrears and closes the file on his case. Blanka makes Selk aware of the problematic background to the art collection. Selk, unhappy as a tax investigator with the closure of the investigation, decides to continue on his own and takes unpaid leave. Blanka appears pleasantly surprised at his interest in the art market and gives him valuable information about its hidden rules. They go to museums, auctions together. In the course of these it becomes apparent that Blanka clearly has her own agenda and her interest in art is not solely academic.

Selk is now operating abroad, with no official assignment and no legitimation. The documents from the German collector put him on the track of the Hirschfelds. He establishes that his secretive but well-regarded firm is operating on the margin of legality. The American tax authorities have also been investigating his business deals, though so far without success. With Blanka's help Selk manages to discover the provenance of a few paintings in Braunschweig's collection—they are works that were stolen from Jews during the Second World War and carried off by the Germans. It was only in the Seventies that they turned up in Braunschweig's collection.

Selk discovers that the pictures went through the Hirschfelds' Paris branch in 1941. David Hirschfeld's father managed to emigrate to the USA shortly before the capitulation of France and save some of his Paris stock. The price for that was that he had to appoint Jumeau, a French employee who was collaborating with the Nazis, as trustee for his operations in France.

The Frenchman was a shady character who not only did business with Goering's agents and the Rosenberg Taskforce but also betrayed Jewish customers of the firm, with whose collections he was familiar, to the occupying power. The loot was shared with the Nazis. One part ended up in Goering's collections, some pieces Jumeau kept for himself and tried to sell them later on the grey market. Important pictures, that it was impossible to sell because they were well known, are still in Hirschfeld's American repository today.

Selk gets into dangerous situations during his researches. He is threatened. Clearly there are other interested parties, whom he doesn't know, looking for the masterpieces that have disappeared. It isn't clear whether they are his American colleagues of the IRS, private detectives or criminals. He is in a precarious situation, since he is acting without permission or an assignment and, moreover, without the prospect of any kind of payment. At one point he is chased and has to kill a man in self-defence.

An ambiguous collaboration develops between Selk and Bianka that increasingly turns into a game of cat and mouse. The sexual attraction is mingled with mutual distrust. Bianka accuses her lover of exploiting her to pursue his own aims. Selk, for his part, suspects she's a fraud who is after works of art that have disappeared for herself. A third aspect of the relationship is the increasing passion for certain areas of painting that Selk has developed under her influence. She has shown particular interest in the work of one particular old master about whom she intends to write a monograph.

Finally Selk has enough proof of the Hirschfelds' complicity in the matter—and he has Bianka to thank for some of the pieces that go together to build up the picture. What remains unclear is Bianka's motivation for helping him. He decides to make contact with David Hirschfeld, the heir and head of the firm. Initially he refuses to negotiate with Selk, so the German talks to Hirschfeld's son, Amos, who hates his father and would most like to get everything cleared up. Amos provides Selk with further pieces of evidence for one of the cases he knows about. Confronted with that, Hirschfeld's initial reaction is to offer Selk hush money, which he rejects. Then Hirschfeld proposes a deal: to return a few valuable works of art to the heirs of the legitimate owners in the one case for which Selk has clear proof. In return Selk is to abandon all further research. Selk insists on giving back the heirs their property himself. At the same time he demands one particular painting from Hirschfeld's store. It is by the old master Bianka is interested in. The art dealer agrees to the deal.

In France Selk gives the stolen pictures back to the heirs of the original owner. They live in Provence and are impoverished, so that in their eyes he is a knight in shining armour. Before that, however, Selk has arranged for an art forger in Paris to make a copy of the picture he made Hirschfeld give him.

When he gets back home he sets a trap for Bianka. He finally wants to be clear about her intentions. He shows her the forged picture. His instinct was right: after a night of sex she has made off with the copy.

Selk has won. All the others have been involved in shady dealing. He goes back to work as a taxman and is promoted. At home in his bachelor apartment he secretly contemplates the the masterpiece he forced Hirschfeld to give him, a magnificent talisman of dubious origin. There is something tainted about the happy end.

Himmler's Hostages

It was only at the end of 1944 that Heinrich Himmler realized that the war was lost. Behind Hitler's back he made an ambitious plan. Through his own agents he made contact with John Foster Dulles in Zurich who was in charge of the operations of the American secret service OSS there. He believed he could persuade the Western Allies to make a separate peace and join the remains of the German forces in a joint attack on the Soviet Union. In this he employed the fiction of a mighty 'Alpine fortress' that he hoped to build up as a redoubt for the SS. He ordered a number of high-profile 'special detainees' to be taken there to be used as a bargaining counter. This true event is the background to the film.

After a chaotic, perilous trek, that took inmates from various prisons and camps through the ruins of the Nazi Germany, a convoy was set up in Dachau concentration camp and taken, heavily guarded, to the South Tyrol. The SS had orders to murder them at once should a serious situation arise.

Neither before nor afterwards has there been such a group of travellers. There were people from 17 European nations among them, including: the previous Austrian chancellor Johann von Schuschnigg; Léon Blum, the ex-president of France; the supreme commander of the Greek army; the ex-president of Hungary; a Prussian prince; generals from the Italian, French, Dutch and Red Army and other high-profile prisoners. Among the German prisoners from resistance circles people from the Stauffenberg, Goerdeler, Hammerstein and von Hassell families, plus industrialists such as Fritz Thyssen, ministers such as Hjalmar Schacht and priests such as Martin Niemöller.

The prisoners reached their destination in a remote town in the Puster Valley. The demoralized SS men were wavering between threats of murder and opportunism.

In this situation two army officers, a colonel and a captain, decide to take action on their own initiative. Forcing the SS to withdraw, they quarter the prisoners in a grand hotel on Lake Prags (Braies) in the Dolomites that went back to the days of the Austrian Empire. The owner is happy to welcome them, even though there is a lack of everything needed to cater for them.

'The locals were amazed when they saw our motley crowd,' one witness recalled. 'Gaunt men in general's trousers, a civilian jacket and slouch-hat, ladies in knee-high army boots, shivering figures with a warming scarf, old gentlemen with shabby rucksacks on their back.'

On 4 May 1945, an advance unit of the American Army arrived and liberated the hostages.

The core of this story is their time by the lake, a grandiose authentic location that is still there today, hardly changed. A script would have to be worked out that was free in the way it dealt with the facts. There would be no other way of showing the interaction between no fewer than 150 people, so the plot would have to concentrate on a few individuals. The following play important roles:

- German General Franz Halder, until 1942 the chief of the general staff, who acts as representative for the whole group;
- Payne Best of the British secret service, who directs the negotiations (he could, if an American producer is involved in the film, be replaced by an American officer) and
- the German Captain Wichard von Alvensleben who forces the SS to withdraw.

In the situation in the hotel it should be easy to develop the obligatory love story. The happy end is effected by the arrival of the American liberators, accompanied by their gaggle of journalists.

The background should be shown not chronologically but by flashbacks: the Reich Security Office in Berlin, the collection of the prisoners from the prisons, secret negotiations in Zurich, chaotic scenes in Dachau, arguments between the guards during the journey.

What is attractive about all this is how, in this idyllic, remote place in the mountains, an old Europe is brought together that at the same time contains a premonition of the new: as well as the brother of Zita, the last Empress of Austria and a nephew of Molotov; Martin Niemöller and a woman who performed in cabaret in Berlin. Above all there were people from many countries, among them were those who had risked their lives in the fight against the National Socialists and wanted to bring about a new Europe, that at the time lay in the distant future.

The course of the taking of the hostages has been the subject of detailed examination in several publications, in particular by Hans-Günter Richardi, who also possesses an archive of documentary material. The Hotel Pragser Wildsee is run by the granddaughter of the owner during he events of 1945; it would, she told me, be available for filming.

Ideas for the Music Theatre

King Kongo. An Operetta.

The operetta is a product of imperialism, which it shows in the same way as it sees itself, that is as unproblematic. The Belgian King Leopold II embodies his age: greed, corruption, exploitation and prostitution, in a word, as the French have it: *La Belle Époque*. This view is the only authentic one and it is essential that it is sustained in the music. Borrowings from Offenbach to Lehár are unavoidable. Nor must the libretto avoid corny rhymes and grotesque material.

SCENE ONE

Brussels, 1878. A crescendo of catastrophic reports comes to Leopold II in his over-ornate private quarters: his secretary explains the internal situation to him: strikes, socialist agitation, protests in parliament against the King's extravagant habits. He realizes that Belgium is too small for a monarch of his calibre and moans about his alarming financial situation. Enter the

Queen Mother and the Queen, who give him a good telling-off, threatening him with a public scandal and having him declared incapable. Leopold abhors his wife. He throws the women out and turns to his mistress, who just presents him with more and more demands for money.

Vocals 1—Quartet: Secretary, Queen Mother, Queen with one verse each, to each of which Leopold responds with the same refrain. Vocals 2—Duet between him and his mistress.

SCENE TWO

Brussels, 1878. Leopold grants an audience to the explorer Stanley who, using a globe, explains the situation in Central Africa, about which the King has no idea. This leaves Leopold cold, but Stanley has also brought a black prince and his sister, in whom the King is *very* interested, much to the displeasure of his mistress. The prince, who admires everything white, is quite happy to hand his sister over to him. He is compensated for this with a Belgian whore; in order to calm her down, the King appoints his mistress as his adviser in questions of finance.

Vocals 1—Duet between Stanley and Leopold. Vocals 2—Quartet with King/Prince/Princess/Mistress.

SCENE THREE

Brussels, 1878. Leopold is negotiating with a consortium of investors who are interested in the exploitation of colonial raw materials. His mistress whispers to him, providing the necessary information and tactical advice. The two of them manage to release considerable amounts of capital. Stanley is called in and given the task of preparing the ground for the foundation of the Congo Free State.

Vocals—Chorus of investors who perform a rhymed raw-materials aria; antiphon about the prospects of making a profit and their conditions. Ceremonial announcement of the setting-up of the 'Independent Congo Free State', a private enterprise of Leopold II.

SCENE FOUR

Brussels, 1883. In the bath the King receives first of all a deputation of Liberals protesting against the imminent proclamation of the royal private state, then the ambassadors of England and France; even Stanley says he has reservations. The King praises the charms of black women, the puritan Stanley is horrified. The African Prince rejects all objections, saying that his country must be finally won over to civilization. The consortium turns up, complaining that the King wants to make himself president and sole shareholder in the Congo company and wants to ditch the investors. The King proposes an international conference that will satisfy the wishes of all interested parties.

Vocals—Chorales gradually getting louder, interspersed with solos for the King and the Prince.

SCENE FIVE

Berlin, 1884. Bismarck has called an international Africa conference at which 14 nations are represented. Africa is divided up in
the offices of the German government. The delegates can be
seen drawing the boundaries of the new colonies with rulers on
a wall map. Leopold, supported in the background by his
financiers, who are speculating on a boom in ivory and rubber,
emerges from the haggling as the winner. His private state gets
approval under international law.

Vocals: A chaotic chorus of the delegates. An argument resolved
by a solo for Bismarck. A harmonious prayer of thanksgiving
from all involved.

SCENE SIX

The Riviera, 1908. The parlour of a high-class brothel. Leopold's
ex-mistress and adviser is the madam there. The girls walk past
the King's bed and, giggling, whisper Leopold's special requests
to the one following them. His personal physician also joins in.
A band, tableaux vivants, a cancan by the whores. In the middle
of all this, two visitors arrive: the Belgian Prime Minister, who
demands that Leopold relinquishes his absolute rule and hands
over the Congo to the Belgian state, and the very old Queen
Mother who is negotiating with the ex-mistress about the King's
will. Leopold, unmoved, refuses to have his pleasures interrupted. During the orgy he has a heart attack. The brothel scene
turns into a funeral service in which, together with his family, the

Congo Prince, the Prime Minister and the delegates of the consortium, the madam and the girls, in tears, also take part. The ritual ends in slapstick: the decorations, costumes and valuables are looted, while Leopold's black servants carry Leopold out of the room on a bier.

Vocals—Chorus of the whores, cancan, the Prime Minister's speech, a duet about inheritance matters. A fanfare during the orgy, a funeral march, jungle drums while the plundering is going on.

EPILOGUE

A platform in Léopoldville, modern Kinshasa. A declaration of independence of the Republic of Congo. Speech by the new president Kasavubu, national anthem, organized rejoicing, Belgium parachutists with machine guns on the alert.

SOME SOURCES

Henry Morton Stanley, *The Congo and the Founding of Its Free State* (1885);

Neal Asherson, *The King Incorporated* (1963);

Hugo Claus, *Het leven en de werken van Leopold II. 29 Taferelen uit de Belgische oudhet* [The Life and Works of Leopold II. 29 Scenes from the Belgian Past] (1970);

Pater Forbath, *The River Congo* (1977);

Barbara Emerson, *Leopold II of the Belgians* (1979);

Stig Förster, Wolfgang J. Mommsen and Ronald Robinson (eds), *Bismarck, Europe and Africa. The Berlin Africa Conference 1884–1885 and the Onset of Partition* (1988);

Adam Hochschild, *King Leopold's Ghost* (1998)

and of course:

Joseph Conrad, *The Heart of Darkness* (1902).

Rosamunde

Poor old Schubert had no luck at all with his operas. It isn't clear how many attempts he made; Otto Erich Deutsch certainly lists no less than 15 from the years between 1814 and 1821, from which there are mostly only fragments left. The number of his failed projects is remarkable. Only two of these works made it as far as a production. The premiere of *Die Zwillingsbrüder* (The Twin Brothers), in Vienna 1820, was a fiasco. It is said that the composer refused to go on stage to face the boos. *Die Zauberharfe* (The Magic Harp) in the same year suffered a similar fate. Both operas were taken off after a few performances and the management refused to pay the composer the agreed fee. Schubert was spared such problems with his later works; they were all rejected, perhaps for good reason but with no explanation.

But Franz Schubert was not a man to let himself be put off by that. He immediately wrote the music for a 'Great Romantic

Play', of which at least ten numbers have been preserved. This
work, *Rosamunde, Prinzessin von Zypern* (Rosamunde, Princess
of Cyprus), had its first performance in the Theater an der Wien
in 1823 and the inevitable happened: it was taken off after two
performances. Schubert's music cannot have been the reason
for that, for even today everyone knows it; the Shepherd's Chorus, the third entr'acte and the final ballet music have really
catchy tunes. And as always with Schubert, the 'rosy cheeks' of
the Shepherd's Chorus are deceptive and that 'The moonlight
shines on the mountain tops' does not mean that the cosy
Biedermeier won the day in Schubert's music—the wind passages in the intermezzos are too heartrending and the Chorus
of Spirits too ominous for that.

In brief, *Rosamunde* is still alive, if only in the concert hall;
and conductors such as Claudio Abbado and Kurt Masur have
seen to it that we can enjoy what has survived of the opera any
time at home. The overture, unfortunately, is missing. In the
music business they therefore resort to a trick and take one
from one of Schubert's earlier works, the disastrous *Zauberharfe*
(D644). Such chutzpah must be allowed, for Op. 26 must definitely not disappear completely from the repertoire.

Who was responsible for Schubert's last great flop? The
question is easily answered: Hermine von Chézy, a lady who
was as ambitious as she was untalented, was the author of the
terrible libretto, which means that every imaginable production
right down to the present day is bound to fail.

Pity, we thought. Together with my friend, Irene Dische, who knows a lot more about music than I do, I wondered what could be done about it. The usual attempts at repairs were unconvincing. But how about a rehearsal which, after efforts that were as fervent as they were vain, mirrored the fate of the original production?

Let us assume that, right in the middle of the Stalinist period, there was a little group of music lovers in Voronezh who had taken it into their heads to put on a production of the fragmentary piece. It is 1936. Voronezh with its 33,000 inhabitants does at least have a university, a newspaper, a theatre, a writers' association and an orchestra. The town is well away from the centre of power; a few officials from earlier times have survived here, among them the theatre director, a Jew who loves the German Romantics. He has a liaison with a young singer with a dubious reputation, whom he has discovered; perhaps she comes from a brothel. She is earmarked for the role of Rosamunde. The project would have no chance without the protection of the local committee of the OGPU. The commander, also a Jew, is a bon vivant; it's only when he's drunk that he displays his occupational brutality. His deputy, a zealot who toes the Party line, has no time for the bourgeois characters he sees at work in the small-town artistic circles.

His caution is not without reason, for the first purges have begun in Moscow. More and more unreliable people are being

banished to the countryside from the big cities. Osip Mandelstam and his wife Nadezhda have been rehoused in Voronezh.
They are more or less destitute but there is no lack of admirers
who make it possible for them to survive, if at a fairly basic level.
The poet is immediately taken into the motley group. He is to
make something of the useless libretto.

Without official permission the big stage is out of the question, therefore the first rehearsals are held backstage, in the
props room or the canteen. Everything has to be improvised: the
scenery, costumes, instruments. Arguments immediately break
out among those taking part and, this being Russia, they are held
in loud voices. Participants loyal to the Party line and malcontents, good and bad performers squabble. Only fragments of the
music are to be heard. In these conditions choruses such as
'How jolly is life in the country' or the shepherds' merry songs
are unintentionally funny.

In later scenes, the mood abruptly changes. First of all,
Mandelstam and his wife are arrested. Perhpas the deputy
commander of the OGPU has a hand in it. Someone probably
eavesdropped on the poems he recited—his famous lines about
Stalin:

His fingers are fat like maggots,
His pronouncements come down like lead weights.
His whiskers are a leer of cockroaches,
The legs of his topboots shine brightly.

At one of the last rehearsals the 'Chorus of Spirits' from Rosamunde, music that is close to despair, is being rehearsed. The music breaks off when armed men come in and arrest the theatre director and the OGPU commander. His deputy has informed on him. Panic spreads. They are all suspected of being Trotskyites and saboteurs. Those who are temporarily spared are left in a Chekhovian atmosphere, in the shadow of fear.

There follows a projection showing Voronezh after it was almost completely destroyed by the Germans in 1942. The curtain falls over a list of all those murdered by Stalin and the Germans. Almost none of those involved survived the Second World War.

Naturally nothing came of this first draft. In the first place we were probably too lazy to develop it. Irene and I ought to have done some fundamental research in Russia and developed a plot that was dramatically coherent. Nadezhda Mandelstam's autobiography, *Hope Against Hope*, an impressive book, was our chief source. But it wasn't enough. We should have known a lot more about Voronezh in the Thirties.

Moreover, we came to realize that there are strict border controls between opera and drama, and that visas allowing you to get through them are seldom issued. Perhaps others will succeed in breaking through the blockade. Keep at it.

Ideas for the Theatre

Marx and Engels. A Revue.

I've always been surprised that no playwright has put this unique friendship on the stage. Goethe and Schiller no comparison! Inseparable comrades and partners in crime, the one a rich factory owner, womanizer and lover of the good life, the other a brilliant exile, bookworm, pauper with carbuncles on his neck, and neither could give up the other, nor their common cause.

Such an alliance was impossible to portray with the bare resources of the semi-documentry theatre that was the fashion in the 1970s. I was thinking more of Don Quixote and Sancho Panza, Laurel and Hardy, Vladimir and Estragon . . . The actors weren't to portray Marx and Engels, they were to *play* them. What follows are the few scenes that are left over from the ruins of this project:

I

An empty stage. A table, two chairs. Working lights.

M. OK then, let's play?

E. Play what?

M. Marx and Engels.

E. That's not on.

H. Why ever not?

E. Marx and Engels are classics.

H. OK then. (*He selects a frock coat and puts it on.*)

E. Marx and Engels are forbidden.

M. I don't believe that.

E. Marx and Engels are anti-communism.

M. Really? Throws him a wig. Now get on with it.

E. Well it's your responsibility.

M. Marx is mine and Engels yours. *He puts on a tie.*

E. You start then.

M. If I have to. (*Pauses.*) *They look at each other in the mirror.* Are you ready?

E. I've been ready for ages.

M. Right then, off we go.

II

M. Sometimes I feel like a dungheap of quotations. Just think of all the things that might grow on it at some point.

E. No cock's going to crow on it.

M. How wrong can you be! I know my Germans, I can already hear them scraping and pecking. Building their nests.

E. Better to burn everything.

M. Oh, let them nose around. If they only knew what's in our letters. That will really scare them.

E. Or not, as the case may be. They'll eviscerate us like the Bible. Something for everyone: professorial chairs, institutes, concordances, indexes. Class warfare as a snowball fight. Throwing quotations, a pastime for professors. An idyll painted by Breughel.

M. What we were really thinking . . .

E. Yes, they would like to know that. We've been working for fifty years and, like anyone who's not a blockhead, we've contradicted ourselves.

M. I haven't.

E. You haven't? Just be glad you don't have to read through all that again. I wouldn't like to study your papers after your death.

M. You can happily leave that to others.

E. That narrow-minded Bernstein. Or Kautsky.

M. They won't notice anything. In fact I prefer political grave-robbers. They simply take what suits them.

E. We'll be their patron saints.

M. Yuck!

E. The democratic, red or even communist lot will never love us. The Russians will prove that we were Russian. The humanists that we meant well. And the Party, of course.

M. As soon as our backs are turned they'll be bashing each others' heads in.

E. It could be even worse.

M. Yes. They even did quite different things with the Bible. A wrong quotation and off with his head. The Inquisition's quite particular about that.

E. I think you're taking us too seriously. I'm telling you, nobody'll care two hoots about us.

M. Sometimes I wish you were right.

III

Engels loosens his tie, takes off his coat and throws it on the floor, pulls the wig off his head, stretches, yawns, drops down into the arm-chair. A sigh of relief. Silence.

M. Now tell me, what's all that about.

E. I'm not going along with this any more.

M. But you have to.

E *(sleepily)*. Why?

M. In for a penny . . .

E. You can say that. (*Sneezes.*) After all *I* didn't put a penny in.

M. But you're in for a pound. (*He takes off his frock coat and hangs it on the back of his chair, takes off his wig but keeps it in his lap.*)

E. I simply can't be bothered any more. (*Blows his nose.*) It doesn't get us anywhere.

M. How do you know that?

E. How do you know that it will get us somewhere? And if it does . . .

M. And if it does, what then?

E. Who knows if it does get us somewhere whether that will be anywhere I'd want to be at all?

M. Why this sudden change of mind?

E. It was my point of view from the very beginning.

M. Really? From the very beginning? It seems to me that you could have let me in on your little secrets a bit sooner.

E. Has that idea never occurred to you?

M. You call that an idea?

E. You imagine you're the only one to have ideas. Presumably something like that's beyond me.

M (*wearily*). Oh do give up. (*Longish silence.*) So what do you suggest?

E. I'm always the one who has to suggest things.

M (*furious*). All right, then. Let's make an end of it.

E. So all at once?

M. You didn't want to carry on.

E. And you maintained that it always led somewhere.

M. You mustn't give up too soon.

E. You're probably thinking it would work without me.

M. I didn't say that.

E. It's not going to be that easy to get rid of me.

M. What are you on about now?

E. I know what you're after.

M. I can't wait to hear.

E. Always looking down on people. Always head above the rest.

M. Oh do stop it. (*Silence.*)

E. I'd have liked to see you—without me.

M. Aha. So that's your line, is it?

E. What line?

M. I'm ungrateful.

E. That's not what I said. (*Pause.*) Either we act together or we don't at all. That's the way it's always been.

M. Yes. (*Pause.*) And these private matters are completely irrelevant anyway.

E. Of course.

M. Right then.

E. Right then, let's get on with it. (*They dress up in their costumes again.*)

IV

Empty stage, two camp beds as far apart as possible. Beside each bed a chair. Semi-darkness. Marx and Engels seem to be asleep.

E. Hey?

M (*half awake*). Yes? What is it?

E. Sometimes I think . . . (*hesitating*) that's not really a life. Always playing a part.

M. What else is there?

E. Well, for you it's different.

M. In what way is it different for me?

E. You just don't know anything else.

M (*scornful*). I suppose you on the other hand know everything.

E. Not everything. (*Pause.*) D'you know, I sometimes feel sorry for you. (*Pause.*) Sorry, I didn't mean it that way.

M (*in a neutral voice*). In what way did you mean it then?

E. Sometimes I feel like chucking it all up and going away. Somewhere or other. Doesn't matter where.

M. That's just like you. And, anyway, it's not as easy as you think. It's not that simple.

E. It is for me. If I want it to be.

M (*sits up in bed*). You've got money, of course. Why don't you just clear off then?

E. So you'd *never* like to chuck everything up and clear off. And if you did, you'd never admit it.

M. Why ever not? After all, clearing off isn't a crime. The number of times I've had to get away . . .

E. I know. (*Sits up in bed as well.*) Then let's get away together then. (*Lies down again.*)

M (*thinks for a moment, then dreamily*). It might be very nice. (*Pause.*) But what then? (*It's slowly getting lighter. He gets up walks to and fro, gesticulating.*) So assuming we chuck everything up and clear off. We arrive, somewhere, we sit around, have breakfast, go for a walk, lunch, a brief siesta, a drive in a cab, and then? What do we do then?

E. I've got an idea.

M. Tell me then.

E. Well . . .

M. You and your dirty habits. (*He puts his trousers on.*) They don't get us anywhere.

E. They get me somewhere.

M. Because you're only thinking of yourself, of course.

E. What about you? I suppose you never think of yourself?

M (*thoughtfully*). No. (*Pause.*) Not when I'm playing.

E (*getting dressed sitting on his bed*). And who are you thinking of when you're playing? Come on, tell me.

M (*quite seriously*). Of Marx.

E. Just of Marx?

M (*grudgingly*). And of Engels.

E. Well, that's something. (*He gets up.*)

M. Of course. You know that very well. (*Pause.*)

E. Right then, let's play Marx and Engels.

They put on frock coats and wigs. Lights out.

V

M. Hey! You've disappeared again. It's starting again any moment now. (*No answer.*) Huh! Just flounces off and leaves me. (*Loudly*) Oh, for God's sake, I can't play Marx and Engels by myself. (*No answer.*) Right then, we'll just have to wait. (*He sits down, drums his fingers on the arm of his chair, picks up a book off the table.*) Capital. (*Leafs through it, shakes his head, puts it away, stands up.*) It's always the same. Can't rely on him. Sometimes I wonder how I put up with him. Right then, let's see if it works without him. (*Mimes the following dialogue*) So where have you been hanging about? With your women? Or are you drunk? You know it's going to start again any moment now.—Here I am. Why are you getting so worked up?—I'm not getting worked up. It's simply not worth it with you.—Then I might as well go again.—Stay a while, there's a good fellow. A cigar? Make yourself comfortable. We've got piles of time, our work can wait, if we don't do any acting today, we can do it tomorrow.—Your irony is totally inappropriate. Since when have you had so little trust in me?

E (*has entered on tiptoe and watched Marx playing out the dialogue*). Is that meant to be Engels?

M. At last! What do you mean, Engels?

E. Who else?

M. You, of course. I'm imitating you, not Engels or someone else. What should I do without you?

E. Right then. If you're imitating me, I'll imitate you.

They swap coats. Marx plays Engels; Engels plays Marx.

E. Why are we actually doing this, Marx and Engels? What's the whole point?

M. Because it's something the people don't know.

E. You don't say! But everyone knows Marx and Engels.

M. The more they talk about us, the less they've understood. Otherwise what do you think things would look like here?

E. In that case we wouldn't be here.

M. All the better.

E. Then we will play Engels and Marx. Why not that way around for once?

M. That's irrelevant.

E. So *you* say.

M. Marx and Engels, Engels and Marx—it's six of one and half a dozen of the other.

E. Long live Marx!

M. Long live Engels!

E. I don't think it's going to catch on.

M. Why not?

E. People won't like it. They're absolutely against us acting that out.

M. There's something true about that. The optimists are afraid that it'll go wrong, the pessimists fear it will succeed. Or vice versa. Some are running away from Marx and Engels, the others are running after us.

E. But if they're running after us, then they're in the right place here.

M. Are you sure? In that case we'd be lumbered with them.

E. All that's too nit-picking for me. D'you know what? If we're not even allowed to play Marx and Engels then I couldn't give a damn about the theatre at all.

M. And if the theatre couldn't give a damn about you?

E. Why don't we ask the people there? (*To the audience.*) Should we play Marx and Engels now or not? (*Confused.*) I don't quite understand. (*Heckling.*) Well if you can't agree we'll just have to take a vote.

M. No.

E. Why not?

M. That's bourgeois parliamentarianism. I'm not going to be part of that. We go on with the play and that's that.

They don't move. Lights out.

But I wasn't happy with these plain and simple dialogues. There was too little action and it all seemed too anodyne. After all, what my two protagonists had in mind was pretty audacious and risky. An old number from a fair, I thought, could serve as background. There, before officialdom banned their act for safety reasons, a couple of daredevil motorcyclists used to race around a ten-metre-high, circular wall. There the Hell's Angels risked their lives while, on an improvised gallery above the show, the onlookers bawled, clapped and made bets about whether one of the riders would crash down.

I imagined that the showman had engaged two riders. The older of the two was to play Marx, the younger Engels. The two men on their roaring machines were utterly dependent on each other. Before the first round they could prepare for the event. After every ride there would be an interval during which Marx and Engels could rest and continue their debates.

As a model for such a production I used an ancient episode from the TV-crime series *Tatort*, which was about a pair of motorbike performers. The actor Klaus Löwitsch, who did his circuits with bravura would have made a wonderful Marx. Naturally no German theatre would even have dreamt of presenting such an extremely dangerous spectacle to the public.

Missionaries

Sometimes you can take on too much.

In 1834 the Reverend Issachar Roberts from Tennessee, a Baptist missionary who had gone to China to spread the Gospel, met a young man in Canton called Hong Xiuquan. The conversion of the schoolboy came about very quickly but his mentor could have had no idea of the consequences it would have.

Sixteen years later, it was this Hong who led a revolt that shook Chinese society to its very foundations. The Taiping Rebellion (1850–1864) was the greatest and bloodiest civil war of the nineteenth century. It is remarkable that this is as good as forgotten in Europe today, for without taking account of the catastrophic event it is difficult to understand much about more recent Chinese history.

The aim of the 'Heavenly Kingdom of Great Peace', that Hong established in 1851 in Nanking, was to overthrow the emperor of the Qing dynasty in Beijing and to replace the teachings of the Buddha and Confucius with what he imagined was early Christianity. His study of the Bible and a series of visions had led Hong to the conclusion that he wasn't an ordinary Chinese but the younger brother of Christ. He developed into a charismatic leader and raised an army of millions that conquered large parts of southern China. The imperial government, humiliated by the opium wars and the advance of the Western powers, defended itself with measures that were as brutal as those of the Taipings. The result was a total war against the civilian population.

Roberts, the missionary, an angry, temperamental man, always in financial difficulties and abandoned by his wife and children, saw Hong as the man who could convert the whole of China to Christianity. In October 1860 he accepted an invitation of the Heavenly King to Nanking. Hong offered to make the American missionary the foreign minister for his kingdom, suggesting at the same time that he should marry him to three Chinese women. That didn't suit the missionary at all, and he kept finding more and more things to object to in the usurper's heretical theology. When Hong demanded that he kneel down before his throne, Roberts finally fled to Shanghai on a British ship. 'Hong,' he wrote, 'is a madman, completely incapable of governing this country.' The preacher had ended up in no-man's-land, between the two sides. The *New China Herald* said, 'Even the man who struck the first match that set off such a raging inferno has finally fled to safety from the monster he invoked.'

By this time the Taiping army had advanced as far as Hangzhou and Suzhou and was threatening Shanghai. Their general demanded that the foreigners leave the city. The besieged inhabitants were close to panic.

Eventually the imperial troops managed to force the attackers to retreat. But it was to be two years of turmoil before the 'Ever-Victorious Army', led by a swashbuckling British Officer known as 'Chinese' Gordon, managed to finally overcome Hong and take his capital Nanking. The Heavenly King committed suicide in his palace by poison and the Taiping rebellion was defeated.

It's obvious that such a huge story could only be produced in the theatre from a very restricted perspective. Let's assume that a few foreigners have barricaded themselves in a bonded warehouse at Shanghai harbour: the British consul general with his wife and his Peking embassy secretary; the commission agent of the warehouse; a Belgian mercenary officer; a woman pianist; a reporter and a press photographer; all with their Chinese servants. When they are joined by the ageing and desperate Roberts, who was in a way responsible for the catastrophe, followed by Charles George Gordon in the uniform of a Chinese brigadier, then we have a view of the uprising which, although European, would be highly dramatic, since all those present fear it but have fundamentally different interpretations of it.

I spent years rummaging through anything I could find about the Taiping uprising. Some fascinating, chaotic, contradictory reading: London 1859; Shanghai 1867; New York 1930; Cambridge 1950; Hong Kong 1963, Seattle 1966; Taipei 1971— and that was only the beginning. But the best of all the books on the subject only appeared in 1996: Jonathan Spence, *God's Chinese Son. The Taiping Heavenly Kingdom of Hong Xiuquan.*

Today, research has made most of the important sources accessible. Only I'm not reading them any more. If I could at least understand Chinese, knew more about missionaries or the way a Briton abandoned by his Empire would think. But that's not the real reason why I gave up trying to put that distant warehouse, that had long ago been pulled down, on the stage. After a heap of notes and draft scenes, I came to the conclusion that the subject was simply too big for me.

Brain Theatre

In the German theatre all human organs are exhibited with the utmost vigour—with one exception: the brain. The inevitable consequence is that members of the audience are more often presented with excreta rather than ideas. Our regret at this is kept within bounds—after all, no one is forced to go to the theatre. And the aversion many directors have for the use of reason is understandable. In their view there are other institutions whose responsibility that is. Clearly we are dealing here with a variant of the mind-body problem philosophers so like to talk about.

However, in the course of time authors keep appearing who are not happy with the amputation of our intellectual capacity. Some playwrights have even occasionally used this talent on the stage and that not in order to bore the audience but to amuse them. Many years ago Brecht provided an excellent instance of that with his *Refugee Conversations*. You could put that play on anywhere, even without subsidies, for it comes without expensive scenery, without video projection and without sophisticated stage technology. Two actors, one table and two chairs are enough. It has little action to offer but any amount of dialogue. It was clearly important to the author that every word could be understood—something of a challenge for some actors whose strength is not clarity of diction.

Other playwrights managed with just one actor. They wrote monologues. Can that be amusing, imaginative, even exciting? Or is it, 'that doesn't work nowadays'? Perhaps theatres that complain about cuts, and they do like to do that, should perhaps have a look at authors such as Lucian, Fischart, Erasmus, Fontenelle, Diderot, Wieland, Lessing, de Maistre, Leopardi, Herzen, Joly or Valéry, or, if that's all too 'classical', at contemporary authors who have a gift for dialogue. A heated argument, a torrential tirade of ideas, a vindictive monologue, a malicious declaration of love—everything would be possible if we could only overcome our fear of our own brain. With material like that the theatre could stand up to any TV chat show. But do we have to? Where would we end up then?

A SMALL LIST OF SUGGESTIONS

Lucian, *Dialogues of the Gods*; *Dialogues of the Courtesans* (2nd century CE);

Erasmus of Rotterdam, *Colloquia* (1518);

Johann Fischart, 'Drunken Litany' (1575)—from his translation of Rabelais;

C. M. Wieland, *New Dialogues of the Gods* (1795)—Zeus and the Unknown Man: Conversations;

Diderot, *Le rêve D'Alembert* (1769), *Suite de l'entretien* (1769); *Entretien d'un philosophe avec la Maréchale de C.* (1776); *Supplément au voyage de Bougainville* (1796)—an argument between philosophers on education and other topics;

G. E. Lessing, *Ernst und Falk* (1778);

Joseph de Maistre, *The St Petersburg Dialogues* (1821); *The Executioner* (1821);

Walter Savage Landor, *Imaginary Conversations* (1824);

Giacomo Leopardi, *Operette morali* (1827);

Alexander Herzen, *Über die Verfinsterung der Geschichte* (c. 1850s)—dialogues from the nineteenth century;

Maurice Joly, *The Dialogue in Hell Between Machiavelli and Montesquieu* (1864);

Paul Valéry, *Eupalinos* (1923); *L'idée fixe* (1932); *Socrate et son médecin* (1935);

Bertolt Brecht, *The Messingkauf Dialogues* (c. late 1930s and early 1940s);

Charles Du Bos, *Conversation with André Gide* (1947) and

Gottfried Benn, *Drei alte Männer* (1949), among others . . .

Ideas for Publications

Dummy

There are people who cannot be persuaded to take out a sub-scription to a journal. Such people will have nothing to do with the reader loyalty on which all newspaper publishers depend. Although we can talk about a certain crisis of overproduction, there are whole teams working on the development of new titles and often enough millions are spent on them.

Both sides could profit from a publication that every month had a brand-new magazine to offer of which there would be only a single volume, that is, its dummy. The editors would be released from the tedious repetition of the same kind of mate-rial. They'd have to think up something new for every month. No regular sections or columns any more, no reserves for the eternal leader writers and no smarmy communications addressed to 'our dear readers'. Even the art director wouldn't have to stick to hard and fast rules; the typographers and illus-trators would really be able to let themselves go, depending on format and size, and show their colleagues what they're capable of.

The purchasers of the journal would never know what was in store for them, but perhaps that would be an advantage; the danger of them getting bored would be less than with all the other printed matter they can buy at the newsagent's.

The Bulletin

'There is no censorship'—true, but things can become pretty awkward for the freedom of the press when unpleasant private matters are made public, when the person exposed goes to court and has more money and better lawyers, when a secret service identifies the informant and puts them under pressure, when the whistle-blower loses their job or the demands for compensation go into hundreds of thousands or even millions.

The questions of power that arise when the results of research into sensitive matters are published are not to be taken lightly. So how about an elegant method of circumventing these problems? It could go like this:

The Bulletin is a circular that cannot be bought anywhere. There is no editorial address nor a 'person responsible as stipulated by the Press Law.' A postbox, let's say in Zurich or Singapore for example, ought to be enough. The anonymous organizers will send their correspondence free of charge and postage paid to selected addresses in a sealed, properly stamped envelope. This means that the contents come under the law guaranteeing the privacy of the post, they are not liable to litigation.

Anyone is free to send a request to the editorial postbox to be included in the list of recipients. Whether it is granted or not is up to the sender; there is no need for a reason to be given. Above all, the mailing list contains the most important disseminators. Thus it only takes a tiny edition to spread the information in the *Bulletin*. The circular does not appear regularly but only when there is enough interesting material.

Possible contributors are any people occupying key positions in politics, industry, healthcare, banking who are prepared, for whatever reason, to blow the whistle but are too worried about the risk of possible sanctions to approach the established media. The *Bulletin* would deal with that concern. Whistle-blowers would be assured that their revelations would be checked, as far as possible, but their names would definitely not be revealed if they did not wish it. An engineer who is annoyed at the deficiencies in safety at an atomic power station, a dismissed manager who thinks his firm's arms exports are irresponsible, a doctor who is incensed at his boss's medical malpractice, a member of parliament who is ignored when he learns of a subsidy fraud, a member of the Brussels Commission who dislikes the secretiveness that is the rule there—they could all reveal their secrets in the *Bulletin*, without endangering their livelihood. Whether their revelations were accepted or not would be entirely a matter for the editors, of whom there would be three. They would, of course, have to deal with a flood of submissions from malcontents and vindictive employees. An experienced journalist will recognize them at a glance or after brief study and consign them to the wastepaper basket. However, the *Bulletin* will not supply proof that will stand up in court, it will be up to the recipients to decide what they are willing and able to put in the public domain.

It is probable that, once the initial circulars have been sent out, word about such a venture will get around if the material turns out to be sufficiently contentious. Anyone who is not among the recipients will, by then at the latest, be asking themselves whether there's something wrong with them.

How realistic is such a project? It is an open question whether three hungry young journalists could be found in Europe who would be prepared to be involved in such a venture that would not only be risky but also poorly paid. For the first two years they would have to manage on a budget of something like $150,000. A single private sponsor would suffice to set it going on a trial basis.

PS: The idea for the *Bulletin* goes back to 1999. It looks as if it was ahead of its time, for since then pioneers of the internet have realized it in their own way. Addresses such as WikiLeaks have shown that it is possible. Only naive observers will be surprised that the potential of the internet can have devastating effects. A community that calls itself 'Anonymous' provides enough examples of that.

The Hundred Pages

Many of the most famous classics are simply not read very much. They are considered difficult, outmoded, not worth the time they demand. People are uncomfortable with hexameters, tercets and *ottava rima*, daunted by multivolume works. Who can honestly claim nowadays to know the *Aeneid*, to have got to the very last page of *Don Quixote* or *Orlando furioso*?

That is a pity. Many of these stories are exciting and have more to say to people of today than they think. One way of convincing both younger and older readers of this is to retell them. By that I don't mean the kind of summary you get in guides to the novel, nor the academic help supplied by introductions, forewords and commentaries, but a literary form *sui generis*, of which only authors who have a solid body of work behind them are capable.

Of course the retelling cannot replace the original, that isn't its purpose. But it can entice people to read it through an approach which, unashamedly subjective, combines a modern sensibility with love of the original. The educational aspect must remain *implicit*. It is true that teachers and pupils will perhaps make use of these, but the enjoyment of reading must remain in the foreground. Any suggestion of a didactic aim would be counterproductive.

What I have in mind is a series of such 'classics retold' seen as a long-term project. For each title an internationally known author will have to be brought in who will decide on the original they feel closest to. The success of the series will depend on the right combination.

We need to define the idea of retelling a book more precisely. It is definitely not an attempt to render the whole of the action of the original. In many cases we would have to proceed *pars pro toto*, that is present only a part of the classic, in extreme cases selecting just one memorable episode. In this we would have to rely on experience of the writer who is retelling the story. To be pedantic would be fatal.

One interesting aspect of the project is the question of author's rights. As far as I can tell there would be no reason to exclude works still under copyright, for it is a matter of course that the reproduction of a story is a distinct form of prose which should avoid direct quotation of more than a few words.

The format is immediately evident from the title of the series: each volume should have a hundred pages. (*Die 100 Seiten*; *Centopagine*; *Cienpáginas*; *Les cent pages*; *The Hundred Pages*; *De hundre sider.*) A hundred pages will not frighten anybody off; they will give one the pleasant feeling of having read a whole book through to the end.

The format should not recall that of school books or the 'little yellow' Reclam texts. A slim volume, taller than a paperback with firm linen binding and a price of €12 to €14—that would be ideal, especially considering that the books could be used as presents. (Wagenbach has shown how successful such a format can be with the Salto series.)

From the very outset this project is only possible as an international undertaking. Alongside the German originator at least three partners in Italy, Spain and France will have to be found. If four such publishing houses get together, then others in Britain and Scandinavia will join in, perhaps followed by some from Japan, China or India and, who knows, even from the country with the lowest proportion of translations, the USA.

There are not solely economic reasons for going about it in this way. Above all it is the only thing that will attract notable authors to the project. The prospect of reaching a worldwide readership with one of these narratives must be attractive even to successful writers. Of course the advances paid must be correspondingly high, say something like €50,000 to 75,000. The first batch should have at least 12 titles and a second batch must already have been agreed. Once the series has become established and acquired sufficient prestige, authors from China, India and Africa, who are less well known in Europe, would naturally be involved in order to widen its literary horizon.

A tentative list of titles:

The Odyssey; Don Quixote; Parsifal; Simplicissimus; The Mahabharata; Jin Ping Mei; The Aeneid; Orlando Furioso; La Presidente; As Meias; Le Rouge et le Noir; Illusions perdues; Gulliver's Travels; Tom Jones; Vanity Fair; À la Recherche du temps perdu; The Robbers of Liang Shan; The Unfinished Sentence; Oliver Twist; Moby Dick; Dead Souls; Anna Karenina; The Idiot; The Brothers Ashkenazi; The Nibelungs; Elective Affinities; The Inferno; Joseph and His Brothers; Under Western Eyes; The Sound and the Fury; Ulysses; The Devil's Elixirs; The Master and Margarita; The Arabian Nights; The War of the End of the World; Paradiso; Dr Zhivago . . .

Possible list of authors would be:

Mario Vargas Llosa; Lars Gustafsson; Paul Auster; Louis Begley; Umberto Eco; Amoz Oz; Martin Amis; Martin Mosebach; Christoph Ransmayr; Per Olov Enqist; Harry Mulisch; Ian McEwan; Cees Nooteboom; Andrei Bitov; Victor Yerofeyev; Daniel Kehlmann . . .

Story

The first periodical of that name was set up by two Americans in Vienna in 1931 with an edition of 197 copies produced on an old-fashioned copying machine. In 1963, the two of them moved to New York where they founded the *Story Press*. The edition rose to 21,000. In Whit Burney and Martha Foley's magazine there were the first editions of work by Charles Bukowski, Erskine Caldwell, John Cheever, James T. Farrell, Joseph Heller, J. D. Salinger, Tennessee Williams and Richard Wright; later there were Carson McCullers, Truman Capote and Norman Mailer. *Story* ceased publication in 1967.

From August 1946 onwards a monthly magazine of the same title appeared in Stuttgart, published by H. M. Ledig-Rowohlt. With the German *Story* the publisher found a yawning gap in the market Ledig published the following authors who were as good as unknown to post-war readers: Isaak Babel; E. M. Forster; Jean Genet; Graham Greene; Ernest Hemingway; Curzio Malaparte; Henry Miller; Alberto Moravia; Anaïs Nin;

Jean-Paul Sartre; Evelyn Waugh; Dino Buzzati; Albert Camus; Truman Capote; William Faulkner; Francis Scott Fitzgerald; Boris Vian; H. G. Wells; Sherwood Anderson; Tania Blixen; Elizabeth Bowen; Ivan Bunin; Jean Cocteau; Ilya Ehrenburg; Aldous Huxley; James Joyce; Valentin Katayev; André Malraux; Victoria Sackville-West; Miguel de Unamuno and William Butler Yeats.

It was a publisher's dream come true. With remarkable intuition Ledig tracked down new writers from all over the world for the ruined country and thus laid the foundations for the Rowohlt Verlag that was set up in Reinbek by Hamburg in 1960. In the early years the issues of *Story* were sold out immediately. The last edition appeared in 1949.

Fifty years later, the German magazine publishers are letting their urge for imitation run riot. The market is flooded with copies and copies of copies—an expensive and risky strategy. Would it not be better to stand back and ask yourself whether there is a gap in the market no one has seen, instead of developing *yet another* magazine for 15-year-old girls or computer freaks?

If you have a look around one of the big bookstores at a station you will see that there's hardly a magazine that has much to it—most of them don't invite you to read but to leaf through them, and you've done with them in about ten minutes. True, there are some more demanding periodicals such as *Foreign Affairs* and *Merkur* hiding in remote corners. But the acres and acres of forbidding print in them are overly theoretical and offer little to amuse one during a four- or five-hour train journey. Of course, you can always take a good supply of other reading with you—there's no lack of whodunits, romantic novels and puzzle magazines.

On the other hand most publishers hate novels and reportage. They're convinced that kind of thing doesn't sell. That is odd for two reasons: on the one hand there's a whole crowd of brilliant storytellers on the world market who use those forms; on the other most people's time schedule doesn't allow them to become engrossed in weighty tomes, quite apart from the fact that most common novels are nothing more than thin plots stretched out over hundreds of pages to suit the publishers. That the periodical market steadfastly ignores such a fundamental need as storytelling is surprising.

A monthly magazine devoted entirely to short stories and reportages with quality writing could remedy this shortcoming. It would ignore the artificial barrier Germans make between 'serious' and 'popular' fiction. A short story by a Nobel prize-winner would be next to an exciting detective story, a report from a centre for brain research beside an insider account of what went on in a Bollywood film. Everything is allowed, from science fiction to classic novellas, plus forgotten stories from the stock of world literature. Excluded would be any kind of literary theory as well as the academic mode.

Such a publication would definitely not engage in competition with glossy magazines. At 128–176 pages, 22 x 15 cm, it could be printed on web-offset book paper. That would mean no colourful series of photos going on for page after page. Particularly good black-and-white photos would be sufficient as illustrations, full-page as far as possible—no postage stamps! Occasionally there will also be drawings, engravings, facsimiles or caricatures. Moreover every issue could have one comic strip, from Töpffer[6] to the *Krazy Kats* and the latest characters, they too best of all in black-and-white. Such measures will not only reduce the costs, they will also indicate the unique selling point of the magazine, namely that there is in fact something to read in it.

It is not only the modest production costs that makes this an attractive prospect economically. The situation as regards rights seems very favourable as well. Since there are hardly any rival organizations looking for the same material, foreign agents and publishers will be interested in using it as a way of making their authors known in Germany, Switzerland and Austria. Thus the editors would have a huge stock of material from all the main languages at their disposal. Only a fragment of the pieces, around 25–30 per cent, would come from the German area, for which substantially higher fees would have to be paid.

Editorial costs would be kept within limits. As editor-in-chief the magazine would need a figurehead, who would have to be found in this country. He or she would not have to do the actual editorial work but would not simply be there merely for

---

6 Rodolphe Töpffer (1799–1846), the Swiss artist who is often regarded as the originator of the comic strip.

decoration—they would give advice and encouragement, make suggestions and objections; someone with extensive knowledge of foreign languages would be needed.

A small editorial team should suffice. All that would be needed supporting the senior editor would be a competent assistant and a trainee. External readers would have to propose texts from all over the world, for which they would be paid when their suggestions were usable. Finally a small group of reliable freelance translators would be needed to prepare texts for the magazine.

It is well known that running a newspaper stall is a cut-throat business but there are still appropriate distribution outlets for *Story*. On the one hand there are the shops at stations and airports and on the other all larger bookshops. It is true that the latter are in general not keen on taking magazines but in this case they would probably seize the opportunity since *Story* means publicity for their core business—a reader who likes a particular story will quite possibly decide to buy a book by the same author from the same shop.

It is difficult to say how many subscribers could be obtained for the magazine. Ultimately that will depend on the extent of advertising. No one can say in advance whether they can make their readers keen to take the next issue. That is only likely if the quality of what is offered is unusually high. There is also the possibility of cooperation with radio stations, appearances on the internet and audio editions.

For the advertising book publishers should be considered first and foremost, since the magazine's readership is an appropriate target for them. There are, however, a few large firms that are involved in cultural enterprises and could use such a medium to promote their image. The inside front cover and both sides of the back cover could also be in colour, in contrast to the dominant black-and-white, if that would sell more copies.

The magazine ought to be operating in the black within a reasonably short time. A high rate of return is not to be expected, on the other hand the project should not be based on long-lasting subsidy from other units of the organization, but the publisher will have to allow for an initial run of at least three years. Setting a shorter time for reaching the break-even point would suggest that basically the publisher doesn't see the project having any chance of success.

The capital investment will be very modest compared with other magazine projects. There will be no costs needed for development, eternal meetings and dummies. At a rough calculation the break-even point will probably be at around 45,000 copies sold at a price between €7.50 and €8.50. That number of sales should be achievable within three years.

It is in the nature of the business that a gap in the market can be defined but no one can say in advance how large it is. The reading public knows very well what it has long had enough of but doesn't know what it has been missing.

Postscript

The Remarkable Rocket

The King's son was going to be married, so there were general rejoicings. The last item on the programme was a grand display of fireworks, to be let off exactly at midnight. So at the end of the King's garden a great stand had been set up, and as soon as the Royal Pyrotechnist had put everything in its proper place, the fireworks began to talk to each other

Suddenly, a sharp, dry cough was heard, and they all looked around. It came from a tall, supercilious-looking Rocket, who was tied to the end of a long stick. He always coughed before he made any observation, so as to attract attention. 'I am a very remarkable Rocket,' he said. 'Suppose, for instance, anything should happen to me tonight, what a misfortune that would be for everyone! The Prince and Princess would never be happy again, their whole married life would be spoilt; and as for the King, I know he would not get over it. Really, when I begin to reflect on the importance of my position, I am moved to tears.'

'You ought to pay more attention to staying dry,' said the Roman Candle. 'That's the main thing, you see.' And she was right, for when the Rocket was to shoot up, he was so wet from all the crying that he couldn't take off.

The next day the workmen came to tidy everything up. None of them noticed the rocket. Only as they were about to leave did one of them trip over him and throw him in the gutter.

Later two little boys came along with a kettle and some faggots and one of them noticed the rocket in the gutter. 'Hey,' he cried, 'look at that old stick down there.' 'Let's burn it,' the other said, 'then we'll get our kettle boiling more quickly.' So they set out the faggots, put the rocket on top and lit their fire.

'Hey, that's splendid,' thought the Rocket. 'They're going to set me off in broad daylight so that everyone will be able to see me.'

'Let's have a little sleep now,' the boys said. 'The water will be boiling by the time we wake up.'

The Rocket was even damper than before because it had ended up in the ditch, so it was quite a long time before it went on fire.

'Great!' it exclaimed. 'I'll go rising up higher and higher. What a success!'

Then, when all his powder had gone, he went 'flop'.

'I knew all along that it would be a great sensation,' he gasped as he went out.

The important rocket didn't get very far, but Oscar Wilde, who thought up this story, lives on.